MW01170057

Ping-Pong Words

And
30 More
Children's Sermons

Marti Kramer Suddarth

CSS Publishing Company, Inc., Lima, Ohio

Scripture quotations are from the New Revised Standard Version of the Bible, copyright 1989 by the Division of Christian Education of the National Council of the Churches of Christ in the USA. Used by permission.

References to *Amelia Bedelia* by Peggy Parish, text copyright 1963 by Margaret Parish, published in New York by HarperCollins Publishers, Inc., are used with permission.

Library of Congress Cataloging-in-Publication Data

Suddarth, Marti Kramer.
  Ping-pong words : and 30 more children's sermon stories / Marti Kramer Suddarth.
    p. cm.
  ISBN 0-7880-2484-1 (perfect bound : alk. paper)
  1. Children's sermons. I. Title.

  BV4315.S79 2007
  252'.53—dc22

                                                                2007024834

For more information about CSS Publishing Company resources, visit our website at www.csspub.com or email us at csr@csspub.com or call (800) 241-4056.

Cover design by Barbara Spencer
ISBN-13: 978-0-7880-2484-9
ISBN-10: 0-7880-2484-1   PRINTED IN USA

Table Of Contents

Introduction

Preschoolers and early elementary-aged children often listen with more than just their ears. They stand while doing art projects, dance while listening to music, and wiggle and laugh while anticipating favorite parts of stories. In short, young children listen with their ears, their eyes, their voices, and their whole bodies! Those of us who teach young children expect this and plan accordingly, using children's "whole body" tendencies to present material in multi-sensory, child-friendly ways.

Young children are very visual, as well. They need to *see* a children's sermon as well as *hear* it. *Ping-Pong Words And 30 More Children's Sermons* makes use of simple props, such as ping-pong balls, helium balloons, and potatoes, to put biblical principles into words and images that young children can understand. Printing Bible verses on card stock allows early readers to see the words clearly and to connect what they see and hear to what God says.

I've learned so much from the children in my life — things that can be discerned only by wide-eyed hearts. The opportunity to teach young children is a gift from God! Open the eyes of your own heart wide; be ready to learn, and enjoy the gift.

— Marti Kramer Suddarth

Actions Speak Louder Than Words

Scripture Reference

"What do you think? A man had two sons; he went to the first and said, 'Son, go and work in the vineyard today.' He answered, 'I will not'; but later he changed his mind and went. The father went to the second and said the same; and he answered, 'I go, sir'; but he did not go. Which of the two did the will of his father?"

— Matthew 21:28-31a

Materials Needed

Miniature candy bars, one per child
Full-sized candy bar
Card stock printed with scripture reference and verses
Assistant

Telling The Story

(Speaker approaches children and calls to Assistant.)

Speaker: Hey, *Assistant*, stand right here. I'm going to give you a present.

(Speaker ignores Assistant and comments to the children about the weather, a current event in the news, a new outfit someone is wearing, and so on.)

Assistant: Excuse me! You told me to stand here so you could give me a present.

Speaker: I know. Don't worry. I'm going to give you something nice.

(Speaker returns attention to the children and again comments on the weather, a current event in the news, a new outfit someone is wearing, as before.)

Assistant: Excuse me, again, but I'm still waiting.

Speaker: I *said* I was going to give you something nice. Why are you upset?

(Speaker turns attention to the children and continues.)

What's happening here? I said one thing, but I did something else. My words and my actions didn't match.

There's a story like that in the Bible. Jesus told it in Matthew 21:28-31a. *(Show card stock printed with reference.)* "What do you think? A man had two sons; he went to the first and said, 'Son, go and work in the vineyard today.' He answered, 'I will not'; but later he changed his mind and went. The father went to the second and said the same; and he answered, 'I go, sir'; but he did not go. Which of the two did the will of his father?"

The father probably was disappointed in both of his sons. One son said he wouldn't do what his father asked, and the other said he would, but he didn't. Neither's actions matched his words, but one son finally *did* what his father asked him to do. In the end, the actions of both sons were stronger than their words.

When what you say and what you do don't match, people react in different ways. Some people will remember whichever makes you look worse. Many people, however, will remember what you *do* instead of what you say.

What did I do today? My words didn't match my actions, and because of that, I might have hurt or embarrassed *(Assistant)*. *(Assistant)* might decide that I can't be trusted. When my words and my actions don't match, I have to live with the consequences of how I make other people feel and what I might be teaching them.

Now, I'm not really so mean. *(Assistant)*, you were a good helper today and you waited very patiently. Here is your candy bar. Thank you for helping me. Let's pray and ask God to help us remember that people are watching us and that we're teaching them about us and about God by what we say and do.

Prayer

Dear Lord,

Thank you for this beautiful day and for loving us so much. Please help us to remember that other people may be looking to us to teach them about you. Help us to remember that when our words and our actions don't match, we can hurt other people or discourage them from seeing you. Please also help us, Lord, to be careful what we say and to be careful that what we do matches our words. Thank you for all of the help and protection you give.

In Jesus' name. Amen.

Give each child a miniature candy bar after the prayer.

All In A Day's Work

Scripture References

A slack hand causes poverty, but the hand of the diligent makes rich.
— Proverbs 10:4

The Lord God took the man and put him in the garden of Eden to till it and keep it.
— Genesis 2:15

Materials Needed

Card stock printed with scripture references and verses, one on each side

Crackers (optional)

Telling The Story

Do you know the story of the little red hen? Once upon a time, there was a little red hen who loved to bake homemade bread. Mmmmm!

To make homemade bread, she needed flour, and to make flour, she needed grain, so she decided to plant a field of wheat. Planting a field is a big job, so she decided to ask her neighbors for help. She went to the middle of the farmyard and asked, "Who will help me plant my field?" And do you know what her neighbors said?

"Not me," said the duck. "I'm too busy floating in the pond."

"Not me," said the cat. "I'm too busy licking my fur."

"Not me," said the dog. "I'm too busy chasing my tail."

"Well then," said the little red hen, "I guess I'll do it myself." And she did.

All summer long, the wheat in the field grew. Soon it was time to harvest the wheat. Now, harvesting wheat is a big job, so the little red hen decided to ask her neighbors for help. She went to the middle of the farmyard and asked, "Who will help me harvest my wheat?" And do you know what her neighbors said?

"Not me," said the duck. "I'm too busy counting my feathers."

"Not me," said the cat. "I'm too busy drinking this bowl of milk."

"Not me," said the dog. "I'm too busy warming myself in the sun."

"Well then," said the little red hen, "I guess I'll do it myself." And she did.

Of course, there was much more work to be done. The wheat had to be threshed to separate the grain from the hay. After it was threshed, the grain had to be ground into flour, and then the flour had to be mixed with other ingredients to make dough. The dough had to be kneaded and then baked to make bread. Each time the little red hen started a new job, she asked her neighbors for help, and every time, each neighbor said, "Not me!"

Finally, the bread was ready to come out of the oven. The little red hen carefully slid the pans out from the heat, and the scent of the warm, freshly baked homemade bread wafted across the farm-yard for everyone to smell.

The little red hen looked at her beautiful loaves of bread and wondered out loud, "Now, who will help me eat this bread?"

"I will!" said the duck.

"Me! Me!" said the cat.

"Count me in!" said the dog.

But do you know what the little red hen said? She said, "I did all the work while all you did was play! Those who don't work, don't eat. I'm going to eat this bread myself." And she did.

That story reminds me of a verse in the Bible. It's from the book of Proverbs, which was written by Solomon, the wisest man in the world. Solomon wrote the book of Proverbs to give us prac-tical advice on how to live, and do you know what Solomon said? It's in Proverbs 10:4. *(Show the card stock with Proverbs 10:4 printed on it and read the verse.)* "A slack hand causes poverty, but the hand of the diligent makes rich."

The word "slack" here means lazy. I know what lazy hands are, but do any of you know what "diligent" means? *(Let the chil-dren offer definitions.)* "Diligent hands" are hands that work hard and do things. They're the opposite of slack, lazy hands.

Proverbs 10:4 is telling us that if we're lazy — if we don't do any work — we won't have anything, but that if we work hard, good things will come to us. God wants us to work. When your

16

mother tells you to clean your room, you might think, "Oh, no! I don't want to work that hard." But God doesn't intend work to be a punishment.

Look at this verse. *(Show the card stock printed with Genesis 2:15 on it and read the verse.)* "The Lord God took the man and put him in the garden of Eden to till it and keep it." God put Adam in the garden of Eden to work! Genesis chapter 2 is very early in the Bible. In fact, it's before Adam and Eve sinned.

When you work, you experience the feeling of accomplishment. You have the thing made or the knowledge that you helped someone else. These are gifts from God, not punishments.

The next time you have a job to do, think of Solomon's words and think of the little red hen. Remember that what you accomplish when you work is one of God's gifts to you.

Prayer
Dear Lord,

Thank you for this beautiful day and for loving us. Thank you, too, for creating us with the ability to plan and to work. Please help us remember that work isn't a punishment, but a gift from you, and help us remember that when the job is hard, you'll help us if we just ask.

In Jesus' name. Amen.

Optional: Tell the children that crackers are also made with flour and give the children some crackers to help them remember Proverbs 10:4 and story of the little red hen.

All In The Family

Scripture Reference

The sons of Noah who went out of the ark were Shem, Ham, and Japheth. Ham was the father of Canaan. These three were the sons of Noah; and from these the whole earth was peopled.

— Genesis 9:18-19

Materials Needed

Card stock printed with scripture reference and verses
Chalkboard or poster board
Writing materials
Family Tree prepared on the chalkboard or poster board in advance
Family History page for each child, copied from this chapter

Telling The Story

Does anyone know what "genealogy" is? *(Let children answer.)* Genealogy is the search for your ancestors. It's the study of your family! Genealogists often keep track of information on a family tree. They start with one person — the root of the tree. Let's make a family tree using me as the root. *(Write your name on the first line.)*

The next thing a genealogist will look for would be the names of the root person's parents. Everyone has two biological parents. Sometimes the person lives with both of them and sometimes the person doesn't, but everyone has two biological parents — a mother and a father. My parents' names are: *(insert parents' names and write them on the tree).*

If everyone has two biological parents, does that mean that my parents have parents? They sure do! Do you know what you call your parents' parents? Grandparents — my grandparents are *(insert grandparents' names and write them on the tree).*

Okay, so we have my name, my parents' names, and my grandparents' names. Do you think my grandparents have parents? They do, and do you know what grandparents' parents are called? They're called great-grandparents! My great-grandparents are *(insert great-grandparents' names and write them on the tree).*

Now, we could keep going with this chart and it would get rather large, but I want to talk about *your* family trees. You see, I've been doing some research and I discovered an ancestor for each one of you. Do you know what his name is? *(Let children give answers.)* It is Noah!

(Show the card stock printed with the scripture and verses and read them.) "The sons of Noah who went out of the ark were Shem, Ham, and Japheth. Ham was the father of Canaan. These three were the sons of Noah; and from these the whole earth was peopled."

That's right. Noah ... as in Noah's Ark! Noah was a real person who lived a long, long time ago. According to this Bible verse, after the flood, no one was left on Earth except Noah, his wife, their three sons, and their sons' wives. That means that everyone who is alive today is a descendant of Noah ... that means Noah is our great-great-great-great-great-great ... I'm not sure how many greats ... many-greats-grandfather!

That also means that every person in the world is a relative ... maybe a distant relative ... but every person in the world is related to you, even if you have to go back to Noah to find that common ancestor. So what should we learn from this?

Number one: When you're reading the Bible, you aren't just reading stories about unknown people. Sometimes you're reading stories about your own family! That makes those stories even more interesting, doesn't it?

Number two: Whenever you meet someone, you're meeting a family member. Whenever you play on the playground, you're playing with family. Whenever you're tempted to be less-than-nice to someone, stop and think, "Is this how I want people to treat my family?" That's what you're doing! You're treating your family member well or treating that person badly. We all need to remember to treat the people we meet with the same respect that we want others to treat our family members because that's exactly what we're doing!

We're going to have a prayer now, and after the prayer, I have a Family History page for each of you. This is a list of questions to ask family members to help you start your own genealogy project. You may photocopy this page as many times as you wish.

Prayer

Dear Lord,

Thank you for this beautiful day, and thank you for giving us family members who love us and take care of us. Please help us to remember that everyone we come in contact with is a descendent of Noah and so everyone we meet is a distant cousin. Please help us to treat everyone with respect.

In Jesus' name. Amen.

Family History

My name _____

I'm interviewing _____

This person is my _____

When were you born? _____

Where were you born? _____

What are your parents' names? _____

_____

Do you have a nickname? _____

When did you get married? _____

Where did you get married? _____

Do you have children? What are their names? _____

_____

_____

What color are your eyes? _____

What color is your hair? _____

What job do you have or did you have? _____

_____

What is your favorite food? _____

When you were my age, what games did you like to play? _____

_____

Do you have brothers or sisters? What are their names? _____

_____

_____

_____

Did you have a pet when you were my age? What kind? What was its name? _____

Where did you go to school? _____

_____

Were you in the military? What branch? What was your highest rank? _____

_____

What is the silliest thing you ever did? _____

_____

What is the bravest thing you ever did? _____

_____

Did you know my parents when they were little? If you did, please tell me a funny story about them! _____

_____

_____

_____

All Things Work Together For Good

Scripture Reference
We know that all things work together for good for those who love God.
— **Romans 8:28a**

Materials Needed
Card stock printed with scripture reference and verse
Goldfish crackers or whale crackers (optional)

Telling The story
Do you know the story of Jonah? It's the story of a *man* who swallowed a *whale. (Pause — if the children agree, continue with the following.)* I'm kidding! Jonah didn't swallow a whale! The whale swallowed Jonah, but actually, the Bible doesn't say it was a whale. It says that Jonah was swallowed by a great fish.

God asked Jonah to go to Nineveh and to tell the people there that they needed to quit sinning and start following God, but Jonah didn't want to do it. So he got on a boat that sailed the opposite direction on the Mediterranean Sea. God knew where Jonah was, of course, and he sent a horrible storm. Everyone on board was afraid that the ship would sink. Jonah realized that the storm was sent because of him, so he asked the sailors to throw him overboard. Then God sent a great fish to swallow Jonah whole. The fish swam around for three days and then threw up on a beach. Poor Jonah was in the middle of it all! Then Jonah went to Nineveh, gave the people there God's message, and the people in Nineveh quit sinning!

Maybe you've seen people swallowed by whales in movies. In movies, the whale's insides usually look like a calm, giant cave. There's a cartoon that shows a man fishing inside a whale, and another shows a man being visited by a choir of angels who sang from the decks of several ships floating inside the whale. It was darkish and damp but not all that bad inside.

In real life, it probably wasn't so comfortable. It was probably pretty hot inside the great fish. And Jonah probably didn't have much room. In fact, it's possible that as he was swallowed, his arm was caught behind his head or his ankle was caught behind his knee. Try it with me. *(Guide the children as they get into cramped positions.)* Now imagine being stuck like that for three days!

You're hot, you don't have any room to move, your foot has gone to sleep, and things only get worse! Our stomachs are full of acids that help our bodies digest our foods. Fish have stomach acids, too. These acids probably stung Jonah's skin and eyes. After three days, they might have started bleaching his skin and may have made sores. It's possible that the acids in the fish's stomach had started digesting Jonah's clothes, leaving them full of holes.

That isn't the worst of it. Fish tend to smell like ... fish. It isn't a very pleasant smell, and if the fish had eaten recently, then Jonah was stuck in the middle of digesting food, which probably smelled even worse. In the movies, the inside of the whale was a very calm, level place, but in real life, fish swim around. Jonah's great fish might have gone up and down and diagonally, making Jonah a little dizzy.

So now imagine Jonah. He's stuck in a tight, cramped place, probably in an uncomfortable position. It's very warm and smelly, and the acids in the fish's stomach are irritating his skin. The fish is swimming around so much that Jonah feels like he's riding a roller coaster with swivel cars. After three days of this, Jonah probably felt sick at his stomach. And then, the ultimate insult — the fish throws up, and Jonah is part of it. Yuck!

The whole thing sounds positively awful, but we have to remember what the Bible says. *(Show the card stock printed with the scripture reference and verse.)* The first part of Romans 8:28 says, "We know that all things work together for good for those who love God."

"All things work together for good" ... can you imagine anything good coming out of all of this?

Do you know what an archaeologist is? An archaeologist is someone who studies other people by studying what they've left behind, and the things the people left behind are called artifacts. Some of the archaeologists who've studied Nineveh think that the people in Jonah's time worshiped a fake god that was based on a fish.

So imagine this: Jonah goes to Nineveh, where the people worship a fake god that resembles a fish. He smells like a fish. His skin is bleached and blotchy. He says he just spent three days inside a fish. It's possible that someone saw the fish throwing up on the shore. The Bible doesn't say, but maybe there were witnesses. And now, Jonah is saying that the God he worships made the fish swallow Jonah, bring him to Nineveh, and then throw up. Can you imagine what the Ninevites were thinking? They were probably thinking something like, "Jonah's God can tell our god what to do! Maybe we'd better listen!"

If Jonah had gone straight to Nineveh, the people would have listened to him. After all, God was in charge. But maybe after hearing about Jonah's experience with the fish, the people listened a little more.

Jonah didn't just make a mistake. He did something a lot worse. Jonah thought about it, and then he disobeyed God on purpose! He chose to do what he did. But God was able to use even that for good. He took Jonah's deliberate disobedience and turned it into a great sermon illustration for the people of Nineveh.

The key here was that Jonah loved God and was finally willing to obey him. And God can do that for you, too. Sometimes bad things happen to us. Sometimes we make mistakes. Sometimes we disobey God on purpose. No matter what, God can take the worst of everything and use it for good. Sometimes we don't see the outcome right away like Jonah did, but ultimately, God will use everything for his plans. You just have to trust him.

Remember our Bible verse: "We know that all things work together for good for those who love God."

Prayer
Dear Lord,

Thank you for loving us so much. Thank you for watching Jonah and for taking even his worst behavior and using it for something good. Thank you for your willingness to do that for us, too. Please help us to be willing to obey you, and help us not to be

discouraged when bad thing happen to us. Help us to remember
that if we trust you, you will use all things for good.

In Jesus' name. Amen.

Optional: Give each child some goldfish or whale crackers to remind them of the story of Jonah and the whale.

Beauty That's All In The Family

Scripture Reference

How beautiful are the feet of those who bring good news!
— Romans 10:15b

Materials Needed

Family pictures — two or three pairs of pictures that show family members who look alike (These may be the family of the speaker or from different families in the congregation.)

Card stock printed with the scripture reference and verse

Feet cut out from card stock (optional)

Telling The Story

It's fun to look at family photographs. Part of the fun is noticing how much family members look alike. Maybe you have your father's nose, your mother's smile, or your grandmother's hair. It can be a lot of fun looking at those pictures and finding out who we "match." *(Show one pair of pictures. Identify the family members shown and point out common physical features.)* When we see these features, we can see that they are related. These people belong to each other. *(Repeat for each set of pictures.)*

Wouldn't it be nice if we could look at pictures to figure out who belongs to God? But we don't have any pictures of God. No one really knows what he looks like, and since God can do anything that he wants to do, he can make himself look however he wants. God probably doesn't have one set face the way you and I do. Since we don't know what God looks like, we can't say, "I belong to God because I have his chin or his freckles." But just the same, if you belong to God, I know what you'll look like. Your hands will look helpful. Your smile will look warm and friendly. Your shoulder will look comforting. Your heart will look big and full of love. And your feet will be beautiful.

You might think that's funny. Nobody — except maybe little babies — has beautiful feet! They're down there on the ground, carrying the entire weight of your body, stuck in smelly shoes or getting calluses from stepping on rough ground. How can anybody say your feet are beautiful?

Well, Paul said it the Bible. *(Hold up the card stock printed with the scripture reference and verse.)* The verse is Romans 10:15b. The "b" means that I'm only reading the second part of the verse. Romans 10:15b says, "How beautiful are the feet of those who bring good news!" Paul doesn't mean that literally. Just because you tell someone about God, that doesn't mean you get an instant pedicure! What it *does* mean is that when you bring someone good news, they're glad to see you coming. Remember, in Bible times, people traveled by donkey, camel, or by foot. When you tell someone how much God loves him or her, you're giving the best news of all. That will make you a welcome sight and give you helping hands, a friendly smile, comforting shoulders, a heart full of love, and the beautiful feet of someone who belongs to God.

Prayer
Dear Lord,

Thank you so much for this beautiful day and for loving us so very much. Thank you, too, that as we try to do what you want us to do, we become more like you. Help us to help other people the way you would have us to, and help us to show other people how much you love them, too.

In Jesus' name. Amen.

Optional: Give each child a card stock cutout of a foot to decorate. Tell them that each time they see the foot, they should think of the *beautiful feet* of Romans 10:15b.

Can I Give Enough?

Scripture Reference

He sat down opposite the treasury, and watched the crowd putting money into the treasury. Many rich people put in large sums. A poor widow came and put in two small copper coins, which are worth a penny. Then he called his disciples and said to them, "Truly I tell you, this poor widow has put in more than all those who are contributing to the treasury. For all of them have contributed out of their abundance; but she out of her poverty has put in everything she had, all she had to live on."   **— Mark 12:41-44**

Materials Needed

Card stock printed with scripture reference and verses
Bag of pennies

Telling The Story

Have you ever looked for a gift for someone but worried that it wouldn't be good enough? Sometimes, we worry that the person receiving our gift won't like it or maybe other people who see the gift won't think that it was good enough. And sometimes, we judge the gifts we receive by how big or how fancy or how expensive we think they are.

In the Bible, Jesus told a story that shows how he judges gifts. *(Show the card stock with the scripture reference and read the verses.)* "He sat down opposite the treasury, and watched the crowd putting money into the treasury. Many rich people put in large sums. A poor widow came and put in two small copper coins, which are worth a penny. Then he called his disciples and said to them, 'Truly I tell you, this poor widow has put in more than all those who are contributing to the treasury. For all of them have contributed out of their abundance; but she out of her poverty has put in everything she had, all she had to live on.' "

Jesus and his disciples were at the temple. In many churches today, an offering plate is passed during the service and people who would like to give money to God lay the money on the plate. In Jesus' time, however, there was a box in the back of the temple.

People who wanted to give money to God put the money in the box on their way in or out of the temple. Jesus and his disciples were watching the box. They noticed several people giving a lot of money. *(Demonstrate the next two paragraphs while reading them.)*

Some of them probably made an announcement, removing their bags of money and shaking them, making sure everyone saw, before putting their coins in the box. Others may have made sure that they held their hands up high and dropped the coins a few at a time, so that the coins would make a loud noise when they fell.

Finally, a poor widow came in. She probably slipped in very quietly, hoping no one would notice, and she only had two very small coins. Of course, we know that Jesus noticed. He told his disciples that her gift was worth far more than all of the money given by the people showing off.

Do you know why?

Jesus wasn't looking at the amount of money. He was looking at the hearts of the givers. The people giving large amounts of money probably had even larger amounts at home. They made a big show of giving and made sure everyone knew what they were doing.

The poor widow slipped in quietly. She gave her money because she loved God, not because she wanted to show off, and Jesus knew that she didn't have anything else left at home. While the people giving larger amounts gave part of their money, this woman gave everything she had. She gave everything because she really loved God.

The money in this story can be a symbol for other things in our lives. When we become involved in church activities, volunteer to help other people, donate clothes and toys, or serve God in any other way, God wants us to do what we're doing because we want to serve him, not because we want to impress other people or because we feel that we must. No matter how much or how little you give or do, to God it's the thought that counts. The love in the poor widow's heart made her gift far more valuable to God than all the other money in the world. When you give anything to God — anything at all — he looks at your heart first. The love for God that's in your heart makes any gift big and beautiful.

Prayer
Dear Lord,

Thank you for loving us and for looking at our hearts. Please help us to remember that any gift given to you out of love is far more valuable than all the riches in the world. Help us to always long to serve you first of all.

In Jesus' name. Amen.

Optional: Give each child two pennies to remind them of the widow's gift.

David And The Giant

Scripture References
David said, "The Lord, who saved me from the paw of the lion and from the paw of the bear, will save me from the hand of this Philistine." — **1 Samuel 17:37a**

2 Samuel 21:15-20 and **1 Chronicles 20:4-7** (the other giants)

Materials Needed
Card stock sheet printed with 1 Samuel 17:37a (reference and scripture) on one side and 2 Samuel 21:15-20 and 1 Chronicles 20:4-7 (references only) on the other side
Mylar helium balloon tied to a nine-foot string with a weight at the bottom
Sling
Traced hand and foot of a six-foot-tall man, enlarged 150%, printed on card stock and cut out
Balloons, one per child (optional)

Telling The Story
Do you know the story of David and Goliath? We can read the story in 1 Samuel, chapter 17, which is in the Old Testament.

In 1 Samuel, the people of Israel were at war with the Philistines. Armies from both countries were camped on the hills overlooking the same valley. Back in Bible times, soldiers didn't have guns or cannons. They fought with swords, bows and arrows, hatchets, spears, and sometimes with their hands, so even though both armies could see each other, they weren't in danger until the fighting actually started.

David was the youngest son of a man named Jesse. Usually, David was watching his father's sheep. On this particular day, his father sent him to take some supplies to his three oldest brothers, who were serving in the army. When David got there, he was surprised to see a *giant* step out from the Philistines' camp and yell to Israel's army. The giant's name was Goliath, and he was making fun of the Israelites. He dared them to send out their best soldier to fight him, promising that whoever won that fight would win the whole war for his country, but none of the Israelite soldiers were brave enough to try.

You might think that David would stay as far away from the giant as he could, but when he saw that none of the soldiers from Israel was volunteering to fight, he decided that he would.

Do you know how big Goliath was? The Bible says that he was over nine feet tall. Have you ever wondered how tall that is? *(Show the mylar helium balloon.)* Imagine that this balloon was Goliath's head. This string is nine feet long. If I let go ... *(let go of the balloon)* ... the balloon rises to about where Goliath's head was. Imagine someone this tall standing in our church! *(Show the cut outs of the hand and foot.)* If Goliath was this tall, his hand was probably about this size. His foot was probably about this size. *(Let the children pass the hand and foot around and compare their to their hands and feet.)* Imagine someone with hands and feet this size yelling that he wants to fight you!

In Bible times, people didn't have access to all of the food and medical care that we have today, and they had to do a lot of very hard, physical labor just to survive. Most people didn't grow as tall as we do today and David was probably between twelve and sixteen years old, not fully grown, when this story took place. *(Invite one or two of the children to stand next to the balloon. Try to find a twelve-year-old.)* Imagine that this is Goliath and that this is David. David walked out to where Goliath was standing, and do you know what Goliath said? He said, "What? Am I a dog and you're sending a little stick out after me?" How would you feel if someone really big was laughing at you and calling you a little stick?

Well, imagine that you're David, facing Goliath. He's over nine feet tall. He's an experienced fighter who has killed who-knows-how-many people already. He's got big muscles, the newest equipment, the best training, and did I mention that he was over nine feet tall? And now he's bragging about how he's going to kill *you*! Are you afraid yet? It gets worse. David was standing there, facing this big, angry, giant and all he had to protect him was a sling and five small stones! *(Show the sling.)* Are you afraid yet? I am, and I'm not even there!

But David wasn't afraid, because David knew that he had a lot more than a little sling to protect him. *(Hold up the card stock printed with the scripture references, showing the side with 1 Samuel 17:37 printed on it.)* In verse 37, after everyone else protested, David said, "The Lord, who saved me from the paw of the lion and from the paw of the bear, will save me from the hand of this Philistine."

David knew that he had practiced using that sling and that he was quite skilled, but more importantly, he knew that he had God on his side. David knew that God would protect him and help him kill Goliath. If David knew God would protect him, why did he gather five stones? Some people think that maybe David gathered five stones in case he missed the first time, that maybe he wasn't quite confident in God's ability to protect him, but that isn't why.

You see, David knew that there were four more giants! You can read about them in 2 Samuel 21:15-20 and 1 Chronicles 20:4-7. *(Flip the card stock over to the other side.)* The Bible calls one of them Goliath's brother and says that all four were descendants of Rapha. Since Goliath was a descendant of Rapha, we can guess that the other giants were cousins or distant cousins. And all four were part of the Philistine army!

When David went out to fight Goliath, he didn't know if the other four giants were in the camp or not. But David had so much faith in God, he believed that God could take care of five giants just as easily as he could one. One stone per giant was enough. If God wanted David to fight all five giants, David wanted to be prepared to do his part.

David shows us that being prepared isn't a lack of trust. It's a sign of faith. David knew that God had guided his training — David had killed bears and lions who threatened his father's sheep — and David knew that God would guide each stone to its target. David just wanted to be ready to do whatever God called him to do.

What does this mean for us? Well, we could sit back and wait for God to miraculously give us the ability to do things we've never done before. He *does* do that sometimes; more often, God prepares us in advance. When we practice our piano lessons, study our times tables, or memorize Bible verses, we aren't doing it because we don't trust God to help us; we're preparing ourselves so that when

God calls us, we're ready. Practicing, studying, and memorizing are all signs of faith.

Prayer
Dear Lord,

Thank you for this wonderful day. Thank you for helping us and protecting us no matter what we face. Please help us to study, practice, and learn what you want us to learn so that when you call us, we can be ready to do your will.

In Jesus' name. Amen.

Optional: Give each child a balloon to make a "Goliath face."

Does God Have Fun?

Scripture Reference
For everything, there is a season, and a time for every matter under heaven ... a time to weep, and a time to laugh; a time to mourn, and a time to dance....   **— Ecclesiastes 3:1, 4**

Materials Needed
Card stock printed with scripture reference and verses
Pictures of the following (look through encyclopedias, children's
    science books, and the internet)
    1. puppy
    2. aye-aye
    3. crocuses
    4. rainbow

Telling The Story
   We're often very serious at church. Helping people learn about God *is* very important. But should we be serious all the time? What does God think about us doing things just for fun? Does God have fun? I think he does, and this morning, I'm going to show you some evidence.
   Exhibit A: puppies. *(Show the picture of a puppy.)* God invented puppies. We know this because the first chapter of Genesis tells us that God created all of the animals, and puppies are animals. Puppies are cute and cuddly and lots of fun to play with ... and God invented them!
   Exhibit B: the aye-aye. *(Show the picture of an aye-aye.)* The aye-aye is a strange looking creature. Believe it or not, it's a kind of lemur. One of its fingers is really long and skinny. It taps on logs and tree branches until it hears the sound of bugs inside, uses its teeth to dig into the branch, and then it sticks its finger into hole and pulls out the bugs to eat! When God created each animal, he thought carefully about how each would be designed. Looking at the aye-aye, it's easy to imagine that God was having fun when he designed it.

39

Exhibit C: crocuses. *(Show the picture of the crocuses.)* Crocuses are flowers that grow from bulbs instead of seeds. They bloom fairly early in the year, sometimes while there is still snow on the ground. Many people love them because they are some of the first signs of spring.

When God was creating plants, he could have made just one kind of tree, one kind of flower, and one kind of bush. In fact, he didn't have to even make flowers at all. God could have created just one plant that would have provided us shade, oxygen, and nutrition, but instead, he chose to create a wide variety of plants. Why would he do that? Maybe God enjoys gardening! Maybe he enjoys beautiful colors and likes to see different sizes and shapes of plants. I think God was having fun!

Exhibit D: rainbows. *(Show the picture of a rainbow.)* After the great flood in Genesis, God promised Noah that he would never flood the entire world again. As a sign that his promise was being honored, God put rainbows in the sky. Every time you see a rainbow, God is reminding you that he won't flood the entire world. Why did God invent rainbows? Could he have created a different sign, one that was less frivolous? He could have, but God chose to use bright, beautiful colors and a big, sky-wide arch. Why?

Exhibit E: Ecclesiastes 3:1 and 3:4. *(Hold up the card stock printed with the scripture references and verses.)* Ecclesiastes was written by Solomon, the wisest man in the world. And what did the wisest man in the world say? In Ecclesiastes 3:1, he said, "For everything, there is a season, and a time for every matter under heaven" and in Ecclesiastes 3:4, he said, "... a time to weep, and a time to laugh, a time to mourn and a time to dance...."

Laughing? Dancing? That sounds like someone having fun! God gave Solomon his wisdom, and Solomon says that there is time for laughing and dancing!

There are times when we really do need to be serious. Helping people learn about God, especially people who don't know anything about him at all, is serious business. But the God who created us in his image took time to rest and took time to have fun.

As you grow, you should follow God's example. Be serious when it's time to be serious, but be sure to take time to have fun, too!

Prayer

Dear Lord,

Thank you for this beautiful day and for loving us so much. Thank you, too, for giving us puppies and other animals, plants, rainbows, and friends, and for showing us that there is time for both seriousness and fun. Please help us to be wise enough to know which is which and to appreciate all you've given us.

In Jesus' name. Amen.

Does God Use Children?

Scripture References

Naaman, commander of the army of the king of Aram, was a great man and in high favor with his master, because by him the Lord had given victory to Aram. The man, though a mighty warrior, suffered from leprosy. Now the Arameans on one of their raids had taken a young girl captive from the land of Israel, and she served Naaman's wife. She said to her mistress, "If only my lord were with the prophet who is in Samaria! He would cure him of his leprosy." **— 2 Kings 5:1-3**

When he looked up and saw a large crowd coming toward him, Jesus said to Philip, "Where are we to buy bread for these people to eat?" He said this to test him, for he himself knew what he was going to do. Philip answered him, "Six months' wages would not buy enough bread for each of them to get a little." One of his disciples, Andrew, Simon Peter's brother, said to him, "There is a boy here who has five barley loaves and two fish. But what are they among so many people?" Jesus said, "Make the people sit down." Now there was a great deal of grass in the place; so they sat down, about five thousand in all. Then Jesus took the loaves, and when he had given thanks, he distributed them to those who were seated; so also the fish, as much as they wanted. When they were satisfied, he told his disciples, "Gather up the fragments left over, so that nothing may be lost." So they gathered them up, and from the fragments of the five barley loaves, left by those who had eaten, they filled twelve baskets. **— John 6:5-13**

Materials Needed

Card stock printed with 2 Kings 5:1-3 on one side and John 6:5-13 on the other (references only)

Telling The Story

The Bible is full of stories of God using adults to do things that he wants done, but does God ever use children? *(Let the children answer.)* Well, you know what? God *does* use children. You don't

43

have to be an adult to serve God. Let's talk about two stories from the Bible that show examples of children serving God.

The first story comes from 2 Kings 5:1-3 in the Old Testament. *(Hold up card stock with the 2 Kings 5:1-3 printed side toward the children.)* Naaman was the commander of the army of Aram, a very important job. Unfortunately, he had leprosy. That's a contagious skin disease. Do you know what "contagious" means? *(Let the children give answers.)* Contagious means that you can catch the disease from another person. So if someone has leprosy and you spend time near that person, you can catch the disease, too. Today, we have medicines to treat leprosy, but back in Bible times, they didn't. People who had leprosy eventually got infections and died. And since leprosy is contagious, people who had the disease were sent away from towns to live. They couldn't hold jobs, so they ended up begging ... they'd live off scraps that other people might throw to them or leave outside of town for them.

Naaman had leprosy. He was going to die. Living in his house was a young girl from Israel. She was working for Naaman's wife as a servant. You've probably heard someone say, "Children should be seen and not heard." The people in Naaman's house probably thought that, too, and it was doubly true for servants. But this young girl cared for Naaman's family very much. She got up her nerve and told Naaman's wife that Naaman should go see Elisha. She knew that Elisha was a prophet of God and could cure Naaman.

There's more to the story, of course. Naaman *did* go to see Elisha, and he *was* cured, but the part of the story we want to pay attention to today is that this little girl was in a place where she could help. She had so much faith in God that she was willing to speak up and suggest that Naaman go visit God's prophet.

There's a story in the New Testament that you've probably heard before. It's told in John 6:5-13. *(Hold up card stock with the John 6:5-13 printed side toward the children.)* Jesus was speaking to thousands of people. All these people had gathered together, but there wasn't any food to feed them! Jesus asked his disciples to find food, but all they could find was a boy who had five loaves of bread and two fish. Now, these loaves of bread weren't like what we buy at the grocery store today. They probably weren't neat, rectangular loaves, cut by a machine, and wrapped in a plastic bag. They might not have been any bigger than a large biscuit even! Maybe all five loaves put together were the size of what a boy would usually eat in a day. Even if they were bigger, they wouldn't have been big enough to feed thousands of people. But the part of the story we want to think about today is that the boy was willing to share. He knew Jesus had asked for help — in this case, food — and he was willing to share what he had with Jesus.

In both stories, age wasn't what was important. God isn't limited by anyone's age. God worked through the children in these stories because they trusted him and were willing to do what he wanted. It doesn't matter how old you are, either. The characteristics that God looks for most are trust and willingness to serve him. Like the children in these Bible stories, you can serve God, too. Whether you are a child or an adult, God can use you if you are willing to trust him.

Prayer
Dear Lord,

Thank you so much for this beautiful day, and thank you for allowing us to be a part of your plans. Please help us to remember that you are always with us and that it's not our talents and abilities, but our willingness to trust and follow you that you most value. Help us to be willing to serve you, no matter how young or old we are.

In Jesus' name. Amen.

Fiction Or Nonfiction?

Scripture Reference
All scripture is inspired by God and is useful for teaching, for reproof, for correction, and for training in righteousness.
— **2 Timothy 3:16**

Materials Needed
Card stock printed with scripture reference and verse
Three nonfiction books such as a cookbook, an autobiography, an
    owner's manual, a math textbook, or a history book
Three fictional books such as a fairy tale, a mystery, a science fiction story, or an adventure
Bible

Telling The Story
Have you ever been to the library and counted all the books? Most libraries have too many books to count easily. Have you ever wondered how the librarians know how to find all of the books? Well, library books are sorted by type. The first thing that a librarian does is decide whether a book is *fiction* or *nonfiction*.

It's easy to remember the difference between fiction and nonfiction if you think about the first letter of each word. Books that are classified (or sorted) as fiction are made up. They are false. They didn't really happen. Sometimes what happens in fictional books couldn't really happen. Other times, the events in a fictional book could have happened, but didn't. Either way, if you remember that fiction is false, you'll remember that fictional books are about things that didn't really happen.

Nonfiction books are about things that really did happen. That's easy to remember if you tell yourself that nonfiction is not false. Nonfiction includes stories about real events as well as books giving you instructions. Either way, if you remember that nonfiction is not false, you'll remember that nonfiction books are true. I have some books with me. Let's see if we can tell which ones are fiction and which are nonfiction.

(Hold up the first book. Read the title and then give a brief description to the children. Let the children guess whether the book is fiction or nonfiction. Tell the children the correct answer and tell why the book fits into its proper category. Repeat for each book. Finally, hold up the Bible. Ask the children whether it is fiction or nonfiction. When the children say that it is nonfiction, ask them the following question:) Are you sure? Do you know what's in this book? There's a flood that covers the entire world. There's a giant. There's even a talking donkey! Are you sure this is nonfiction? *(Let the children answer again.)*

You know what? The Bible is nonfiction. It's not false. It's true. The Bible is different than other books because it's the word of God. That means that God gave the words to human writers to write down, but the words belong to God.

(Show the card stock printed with the scripture reference and read the verse.) 2 Timothy 3:16 tells us "All scripture is inspired by God and is useful for teaching, for reproof, for correction, and for training in righteousness."

This verse means that God himself created words in the Bible, that all of them are true, and that all can help us learn to be the kind of people God wants us to be. In the Bible, we find adventure, mystery, intrigue, poetry, and more. But most importantly, we find God speaking to us, thousands of years after the words were written. The Bible definitely is nonfiction because the Bible is definitely true.

Prayer
Dear Lord,

Thank you so much for sending us the Bible. Please help us to remember that the Bible is your message to us, and help us to use it to learn more about you and how to be the kind of people you want us to be.

In Jesus' name. Amen.

Football Versus Love
(for a Sunday between the Super Bowl and Valentine's Day)

Scripture Reference

Love is patient; love is kind; love is not envious or boastful or arrogant or rude. It does not insist on its own way; it is not irritable or resentful; it does not rejoice in wrongdoing, but rejoices in the truth. It bears all things, believes all things, hopes all things, endures all things. Love never ends. **— 1 Corinthians 13:4-8a**

Materials Needed

Football
Heart-shaped candy box or piece of construction paper
Card stock printed with scripture reference and verses
Heart-shaped candy (optional)

Telling The Story

What's this? *(Show the football and let the children answer.)* It's a football, and it's used to play a game called football.

What's this? *(Show the heart.)* It's a heart. The heart beating inside your body isn't really shaped like this, but we call this a heart shape, and it's often used to remind us of love.

Every winter, usually late in January or very early in February there's a very famous football game played on television. This year it was on *(date)*. Does anyone know what it's called? *(Let the children answer.)* It's called the Super Bowl, and the Super Bowl is all about football. Coming up is a holiday that's all about love. It's on February 14. Can anyone tell me what that day is? *(Let the children answer.)* That's right! It's Valentine's Day, and Valentine's Day is all about love.

The Super Bowl is about football, and Valentine's Day is about love. Football ... and love. Can football teach us anything about how God wants us to love each other? What if we talk about how football and love are different?

When you play football, there are two teams. If you look at the scoreboard, the team names might be listed, or maybe the scoreboard says, "Home" and "Visitor." Either way, there are two teams and each team is divided into two squads: The offense and the defense. The offense tries to score points and the defense tries to stop the offense of the other team.

In love, we work together. Whether we're talking about the love you feel for a friend, the love you feel for someone in your family, or a boyfriend and girlfriend kind of love, there is only one team. When you love someone you work for each other, not against each other. God wants us to work together.

When people play football, they're always trying to knock other people down. Two players run into each other, and knock or pull each other to the ground. It's called tackling, and it is part of the game. But when you love someone, you try to build that person up. How do you build other people up? You help them. You do nice things for them and encourage them. So football and love are opposites in that sense. In football, you knock people down. In love, you build them up. God wants us to build each other up.

There's something else different about football and love. In football, there are a lot of rules! There are rules about how long you can hold the ball, who you can throw it to, when you can move and when you can't, who you can tackle and who you can't, what you can do if you do have the ball, and what you can do if you don't. It's very complicated. The rulebook is thick, too!

Love, on the other hand, doesn't have big set of rules. God asks us to love him first and then to love the people around us the way we love ourselves. That's a lot easier to remember, and we don't need a referee to help us because we've got God. There are many complicated rules in football, but only two, simple things God want us to remember about love: Love God first and love our neighbors as ourselves.

There's something else. Football is played with a timer, and you know what? The referee is always stopping the timer. In fact, it seems like a football game is only played for five or ten seconds at a time, and then someone breaks one of those complicated rules we just talked about, and the referee stops the game and the timer.

Love isn't like that. There's no time limit, and you don't stop and start love again and again. When you love someone, you love that person all the time, the way God loves us. Even if the person makes a mistake, you love that person anyway, because God wants us to love all the time.

The differences between love and football aren't just sentiments made up by greeting card companies. They're found in the Bible! Paul, who wrote much of the New Testament, wrote about love in a very famous set of verses that you've probably heard read at a wedding. *(Show the card stock with the printed scripture reference and verses.)*

In 1 Corinthians 13:4-8a, Paul wrote: "Love is patient; love is kind; love is not envious or boastful or arrogant or rude. It does not insist on its own way; it is not irritable or resentful; it does not rejoice in wrongdoing, but rejoices in the truth. It bears all things, believes all things, hopes all things, endures all things. Love never ends."

Do you know what these verses mean? They're talking about the biggest difference between football and love. In football, the object of the game is to get the most points. To win the game, your team needs the biggest score.

But in love, no one is trying to win. According to 1 Corinthians 13:4-8a, love doesn't keep score. God doesn't want us to keep score with the people that we love, and most importantly, God doesn't keep score with us. If you love God and you are trying to do what he wants you to do, he'll forgive and forget your sins and love you with all his heart. That's what God wants us to do with the people we love, too.

Prayer

Dear Lord,

Thank you for this beautiful day, and thank you for loving us so much and for giving us the Bible to help us learn what you want us to do. Please help us to be patient and kind with the people around us, and help us to remember not to "keep score."

In Jesus' name. Amen.

Optional: Give children heart-shaped pieces of candy.

Handmade By God

Scripture Reference
Before I formed you in the womb I knew you. — **Jeremiah 1:5a**

Materials Needed
Card stock printed with scripture reference and verse, with the words "I formed you" underlined

Telling The Story

Have you ever had a really bad day? You wake up late. There's no hot water left for your shower, and your favorite cereal is all gone, so you have to eat something you don't like for breakfast. Halfway to school, you realize that when you were brushing your teeth, you missed a spot, and now you have to spend the rest of the day with morning breath. After you get to school, you discover that you forgot to do your homework, but that doesn't matter because the juice box that you packed in your lunch leaked and now everything in your backpack is soaked. One of your teachers gives a pop quiz, and during gym, you're the last one chosen for a kickball team. Your best friend won't speak to you. On the way home, you drop your art project. When you get home, you spill your milk while eating your after-school snack, and worst of all, even your dog won't play with you.

What a rotten day. We all have days like that, and when we do, it's easy to start thinking that maybe something is wrong with us. Maybe we're stupid. Maybe we think something even worse. On days like that, we need to remember Jeremiah 1:5a. *(Hold up the card stock printed with the scripture reference and verse.)* The reason this card says verse 5a is because I'm just reading the first part of the verse. "Before I formed you in the womb, I knew you."

God is talking to Jeremiah in this verse, but he's talking to us, too. God made Jeremiah. God made each one of us, too. Look at the underlined words: "I formed you." We aren't accidents. We aren't by-products. God formed each and every one of us. He planned us and made us himself ... on purpose.

Look at the words at the end of this sentence: "I knew you." Each one of us is so special to God that he took the time to get to know us even before we were made! Each one of you is so special that God even keeps track of how many hairs are growing out of your head. When you comb your hair in the morning and a few hairs fall out and stick in the comb, God even keeps track of that. He does this because he loves you very much.

Even on the worst day of your life, even when you feel like no one cares, it's important to remember that God loves you very much and you are very special to him. That's why he sent his Son to die for each one of us. No matter how bad a day may seem, it's a good day because God loves you very much.

Prayer
Dear Lord,

Thank you so much for loving us. Thank you for hand-making each one of us and loving us so much that you count our hairs. Please help us, even on the worst of our bad days, to remember how much you care and help us to be able to share that love with the people around us.

In Jesus' name. Amen.

Having Or Doing?

Scripture Reference

Do not store up for yourselves treasures on earth, where moth and rust consume, and where thieves break in and steal; but store up for yourselves treasures in heaven, where neither moth nor rust consumes, and where thieves do not break in and steal. For where your treasure is, there your heart will be also.

— Matthew 6:19-21

Materials Needed

Card stock printed with scripture reference and verses, with the words, "For where your treasure is, there your heart will be also" underlined

Telling The Story

Have you ever asked someone who is the age of your grandparents or great-grandparents what life was like when he or she was a child? If you have, then maybe you noticed that the person talked more about the things he did or the people he spent time with than about the things that he had. Many people remember what they *do* better than what they *have* (or *had*), and they enjoy those memories better. Why do you think that might be? *(Let children offer guesses.)*

Those are great ideas. I think it's because what you *do* often involves other people. When you do something, you often share that time with other people. When you have something, you might share it with other people, but that *sharing* means you're doing something, doesn't it? If you just have something, you might do something with it or you might just sit and look at it alone. Things just don't stay in our memories or create pleasant memories as well as actions and relationships do.

The Bible tells us about this in Matthew 6:19-21. *(Show the card stock with the printed scripture reference and verses and read the verses.)* It says, "Do not store up for yourselves treasures on earth, where moth and rust consume, and where thieves break in and steal; but store up for yourselves treasures in heaven, where neither moth nor rust consumes, and where thieves do not break in and steal. For where your treasure is, there your heart will be also."

Jesus tells us that things wear out. They can be broken or stolen. But our relationship with God — our biggest treasure in heaven — is forever. It will never wear out, never break, and never be stolen. And when we do things for God, he remembers. God's memory is forever, too.

What happens if you have a lot of toys? You have a messy room. You have many things that need to be dusted and taken care of. You worry that they'll get broken, and sometimes they're even in the way. Things can be fun to have, but they bring their own problems with them.

What happens if you spend time doing things with and for other people? You teach them, and you learn from them. You exercise your brain and feel the satisfaction of helping. And as you get to know people, you make friends that you can turn to when you have a problem, too.

Remember what Matthew 6:21 says. It's underlined on this card. *(Hold up the card stock again.)* "For where your treasure is, there your heart will be also." That means, if you are more concerned with getting *things*, someday your heart will be at the dump, because that's where the broken things end up. When you're alone, you won't have great memories to help you, and maybe someday, you won't even have much to remember.

If you are more concerned with doing things with other people, you exercise your brain, make your memory stronger, and you look forward to seeing those people in heaven, which is forever.

Prayer
Dear Lord,

Thank you for this beautiful day, and thank you for helping us realize that our hearts will focus on whatever we treasure. Please help us to remember that our real treasures are waiting for us in heaven, not at the store or at home in our rooms. Thank you for loving us so much.

In Jesus' name. Amen.

If You're Angry

Scripture Reference
If another member of the church sins against you, go and point out the fault when the two of you are alone. If the member listens to you, you have regained that one. **— Matthew 18:15**

Materials Needed
Card stock printed with scripture reference and verse
Assistant

Telling The Story
Speaker: I am so mad! Boy, am I mad! Do you want to hear about it? I am so mad. And do you know who I'm mad at? I'm mad at Ignatz! Ignatz Rockabalsky, that's who! That Ignatz! He made me so mad and when I tell you what he did, you'll be mad at him, too. Do you know what he did? You see, he ...

Assistant: *(interrupts)* Wait a minute! Should you be telling *us* why you're mad?

Speaker: What do you mean?

Assistant: Well, maybe you should be talking to Ignatz instead of us.

Speaker: But I don't want to talk to Ignatz. I'm mad at him. I'd much rather tell all of you all about it.

Assistant: I know, but what does the Bible say about being mad?

Speaker: I don't know.

Assistant: I do. It's written on this card. *(holds up card stock with scripture reference and reads the verse)* "If another member of the church sins against you, go and point out the fault when the two of you are alone. If the member listens to you, you have regained that one." That's from Matthew 18:15.

Speaker: You're right. Sometimes we get mad at people. It happens, and God understands. It isn't a sin to get angry, but what we *do* about that anger is important. Sometimes it's fun to be angry, isn't it? You get to be the center of attention when you tell everyone about it. You get to claim that you'd never do such a thing. (We call that "righteous indignation.") But that isn't what Jesus wants us to do, is it?

Imagine Ignatz, again. What if Ignatz didn't realize that the thing he did would hurt my feelings? What if he didn't even do the thing that I think he did? If I talk about him behind his back, instead of giving Ignatz a chance to apologize or to explain, I'm putting him in a place where he feels that he has to defend himself and "save face." I'm angry, Ignatz is angry, and that just makes both of us even more angry. The situation will probably get worse. Do you think that's what Jesus wants?

In Matthew 18:15, Jesus tells us what we should do if we are angry with someone. He doesn't want us to gossip or sit and stew. Jesus wants us to either forgive and forget or else talk to the person, one-on-one, and try to work things out. If I go talk to Ignatz, he might feel sorry for hurting my feelings, or I might discover that he isn't even guilty! We have the chance to talk and come up with a solution to the problem instead of making a new one.

Now, Ignatz and I are both human. We might talk and still not be able to work things out, but Jesus talks about that, too. If you continue reading Matthew 18, Jesus tells you what to do if talking one-on-one doesn't work. Jesus still has a plan!

But for today, the thing to remember is that Jesus wants us to talk to the person we're mad at instead gossiping with everyone else. And if talking to the person is hard, remember that Jesus will help you.

Prayer

Dear Lord,

Thank you so much for this beautiful day and for your words of wisdom in Matthew 18. Please help us not to gossip, and help us to talk with the person we're angry with. Please give us the wisdom we need to do what you want us to do. Thank you for your help when what you want us to do is difficult.

In Jesus' name. Amen.

A Lamp To My Feet

Scripture Reference
Your word is a lamp to my feet and a light to my path.

— Psalm 119:105

Materials Needed
Flashlight
Sheet of black construction paper (optional)
Card stock printed with scripture reference and verse

Telling The Story
(Hold up the flashlight.) What is this? *(Allow the children to answer.)* That's right. It's a flashlight. A flashlight uses batteries and a small light bulb to create a light, like this. *(Shine flashlight. Shine it on the construction paper if there is too much light to see the light on the carpet or floor.)*

As you might imagine, this flashlight really comes in handy. Imagine that I'm camping. It's the middle of the night, and I wake up and realize that I need to go to the bathroom. The problem is that it's dark outside! What do I do? I grab my trusty flashlight and shine it on the path between my tent and the outhouse. *(Shine the flashlight on the floor or on the construction paper to simulate shining the flashlight on the path.)*

I walk along, looking at the path in the light. Suddenly, I see a rock. I don't want to stub my toe, so I walk around the rock. A few steps later, I see a large tree root. I don't want to trip and fall, but thanks to my flashlight, I see the root in plenty of time. I'm able to step over the root without falling. I keep walking, when suddenly, I see a skunk in the middle of the path! The last thing I want to do is scare a skunk. So I back up and wait for the skunk to cross the path and then I proceed. Good thing I have my trusty flashlight. The light that comes from my flashlight helps me safely walk down the path and avoid getting hurt or lost.

This flashlight reminds me of a verse in the Bible. *(Hold up the card stock with the scripture reference and verse printed on it.)*

It's Psalms 119:105: "Your word is a lamp to my feet and a light to my path."

"Your word is a lamp to my feet ..." Does that mean that the next time I go camping, I don't need to take a flashlight? Can I just use my Bible instead? No. This verse is using symbolism. One thing stands for or represents another.

The *path* in this verse represents my life. My *feet* in this verse represent me living my life. If I think of myself walking down a path, I have a symbol of me living my life, doing the things I do, and making the decisions that I make.

In Bible days, people didn't have battery-operated flashlights. When David wrote this verse, he was probably thinking about an oil lamp of some sort. *Your word* in this verse really does mean God's word or the Bible, but when the verse says that God's word is a *lamp*, it doesn't literally mean that we can use it like an oil lamp or a flashlight. Instead, it means that the Bible provides guidance. It shows me things that might cause me to sin and it helps me make decisions, just like the flashlight showed me things on the path that might cause me to trip and fall or to scare a skunk. If the path is a symbol for my life, then the lamp or light represents the Bible showing me how to safely walk that path.

Prayer
Dear Lord,

Thank you so much for loving us and for giving us the Bible to help us as we navigate the world around us. Thank you for guiding us. Please help us to remember that the Bible is your gift to us.

In Jesus' name. Amen.

Like A Potato

Scripture Reference
The gifts he gave were that some would be apostles, some prophets, some evangelists, some pastors and teachers.

— **Ephesians 4:11**

Materials Needed
Three potatoes
Card stock printed with scripture reference and verse

Telling The Story
I'd like to show you something. Does anyone know what this is? *(Show a potato. Let the children answer.)* That's right. It's a potato! I love potatoes! Potatoes taste good. They're full of vitamins and minerals that help us stay healthy, and there are many different ways we can cook potatoes.

One of my favorite ways to eat a potato is to bake it. I love baked potatoes. I bake it at 425 degrees for an hour, split it open, and top it with *(list your favorite potato toppings)*. Mmm ... that sounds good. In fact, it sounds so good that I think I'll take this potato home and bake it for supper. *(Set the potato aside, where the children can see it.)*

I'd like to you show something else. *(Show the second potato.)* Does anyone know what this is? *(Let the children answer.)* That's right! It's a potato! I love potatoes. They taste good, they're full of vitamins and minerals that help us stay healthy, and there are many different ways we can cook them.

One of my other favorite ways to eat a potato is to mash it. I peel the potato, boil it in water for twenty minutes, drain off the water, add a little milk and a little butter, and then mash the potatoes with my hand mixer. Sometimes I eat mashed potatoes with gravy and sometimes I eat them plain. Usually I cut up my meat and dip each bite in the mashed potatoes. Mashed potatoes are so good. In fact, that sounds so good that I think I'll take this potato home and make mashed potatoes for supper tomorrow. *(Set the potato next to the first potato, where the children can see both.)*

I'd like to show you something else. *(Show the third potato.)* Does anyone know what this is? *(Let the children answer.)* That's right! It's a potato! I love potatoes. They taste good, they're full of vitamins and minerals that help us stay healthy, and there are many different ways we can cook them.

Another way that I like to eat potatoes is to make hash browns. Now, hash browns aren't quite as good for me as baked potatoes and mashed potatoes. Hash browns have to be fried in grease or vegetable oil, which adds a little fat to them. But I still like to eat them. In fact, hash browns sound so good that I think I'll take this potato home and make hash browns for supper the day after tomorrow. *(Set this potato by the other two, where the children can see them.)*

Here we have three potatoes. Do you know what the amount of food you eat at one time is called? *(Let the children answer.)* It's called a "serving." Probably that name came from the fact that when someone gives you some food, they serve you, but there's another way we could think of it. Remember the vitamins and minerals that I said are in the potato. We could think of the potato as serving whoever eats it. It serves you or me by giving us the nutrition that we need. The potato is serving me when I eat it for supper.

How are people like potatoes? *(Let the children offer some answers.)* All those are good ideas, but there's another way.

Remember the potato? It serves me by giving me nutrition, but it can do that in many different ways. I could bake it, mash it, fry it, and I can cook the potato in other ways, too. There are many different ways the potato can serve me. Potatoes serve people, and people serve God. But guess what? There are many different ways that we can serve God. Who has some ideas? *(Let the children suggest ways that people can serve God.)* That's great! You've thought of a lot of ways we can serve God. Those ways are all different, but they're all important, and they all ultimately serve God.

(Hold up the card stock with the scripture reference and verse printed on it.) Paul, who wrote much of the New Testament, gives us some ideas, too. In Ephesians 4:11, he wrote, "The gifts he gave were that some would be apostles, some prophets, some evangelists, some pastors and teachers." These are just some of the ways

that Paul says we can serve God. They're all different and they all ultimately serve God.

Now, how are people different than potatoes? *(Let the children offer some answers.)* Very good! Those are all ways we are different than potatoes, but there is another very important way.

Remember the potato? It can only serve one person, one way, and only one time. After I eat this potato, it'll be gone. I can never eat it again. But people aren't like that. Each one of us can serve God many times and many different ways. In fact, God will probably ask you to serve him different ways at different times in your life. The important things to remember are that:

1. Everyone is able to serve God — so never think that you can't.
2. God is never "done" with you. God is always able to use you, even when you think you don't have any abilities, even if someday you think you're too old, or too tired. Even if you think you've sinned so badly that God won't ever want to hear from you ever again, he still loves you and will still use you if you let him.

So always be alert for ways that you can serve God and always be listening for God's directions, and then you can serve God, like a potato!

Prayer:
Dear Lord,

Thank you for this beautiful day, and thank you for making potatoes that give us some of the nutrition we need. Please help us to remember that we can serve you in many different ways and help us to see how you want each of us, as individuals, to serve. Thank you for guiding us.

In Jesus' name. Amen.

65

Like Iron Sharpens Iron

Scripture Reference
Iron sharpens iron, and one person sharpens the wits of another.
— **Proverbs 27:17**

Materials Needed
Card stock printed with scripture reference and verse
Assistant

Telling The Story
Good morning! I'd like to introduce you to my friend, *(name)*. *(Name)* and I met *(where and when)*. Do you know what I like about *(name)*? *(List three or four things about the assistant.)* Something else special about *(name)* is that if I asked him/her to pray for me, I know that he/she would. He/she helps me grow closer to God because he/she is close to God. When I see *(name)* doing what God wants him/her to do, then I'm encouraged to do what God wants me to do, too.

You've probably heard the story of Solomon. After Solomon became king of Israel, God made Solomon the wisest man in the world. Do you know what the wisest man in the world says about friends? *(Show card stock and printed with scripture reference and verse and read it.)* In Proverbs 27:17, he wrote, "Iron sharpens iron, and one person sharpens the wits of another."

Iron is a sturdy metal that is used to make beams for buildings, tools, furniture, and more. An ironworker might heat the metal to make it softer or use one piece of metal to sharpen another piece to make an axe or a blade for a plow. In this verse, Solomon is comparing the way two pieces of ironwork together to the way two people influence each other.

Proverbs 27:17 is an amazing verse because it's both a promise and a warning. Solomon realized that the people around us have a great influence on us. Sometimes we don't get to choose who we spend time with, but when we do, we need to be careful.

Christian friends, like *(name)*, will help us grow closer to God because they'll pray for us. Sometimes we study about God together. Even when we aren't studying or praying together, our Christian friends won't suggest doing sinful things together. Think about a Christian person you know. Has that person ever suggested robbing a bank together? No.

Proverbs 27:17 promises us that if we spend time with people who are following God, those people will influence us to be followers of God. People who don't follow God can sometimes pull us away from God. Imagine someone offering you drugs or suggesting that you shoplift from a local store. Sometimes their suggestions pull us away from God more slowly, but they still pull us away. What would you do if a friend invited you to watch a television program that you know God doesn't want you to watch?

Proverbs 27:17 warns us that people who don't follow God pull us away and that we need to be very careful about their influence. Does this mean that you shouldn't be friends with someone who doesn't follow God? No. Remember that Proverbs 27:17 is a promise, too. Just as our Christian friends influence us to follow God, we can influence our friends to follow God. We just have to be careful with those friendships.

Instead of going to a friend's house when you know that friend is alone, invite your friend to your house when your parents are home to supervise. Ask your friend to come along when a group of Christian friends are doing something together or to an activity at church. Suggest a different television show. Loan your friend a book that your parents have approved. Talk to your parents or your pastor or your Sunday school teacher if a friend asks you to do something that makes you uncomfortable. If you're careful about your friendship, then you can be the "iron" that sharpens your friend.

Prayer
Dear Lord,

Thank you for this beautiful day, and thank you for giving Solomon the wisdom that he shares with us in the book of Proverbs. Please give us the wisdom to look for friends who will help us to grow closer to you and to be a good influence on our friends, too. Please also help us to know when to ask another person for help with a friendship so that we can careful not to be pulled away from you. Thank you for loving and helping us so much.

In Jesus' name. Amen.

Love Your Neighbor As Yourself

Scripture Reference

Love your neighbor as yourself.   **— Matthew 22:39b**

Materials Needed

Amelia Bedelia book by Peggy Parish

Card stock printed with scripture reference and verse

Telling The Story

Have you ever noticed that some words have more than one meaning? They can mean different things, depending on the way we use them, and sometimes, that can cause a little confusion. *(Show the cover of* Amelia Bedelia.*)* Many of you have probably read this book. It's called *Amelia Bedelia*, and it was written by Peggy Parish. This book is fun because the main character, Amelia Bedelia, gets a little confused by words that mean more than one thing.

(Open the book to the first page and show the children.) Amelia Bedelia is starting a new job cooking and cleaning for the Rogers family. They have to be out of the house on her first day, so they leave her a list of things to do. The fun starts when Amelia Bedelia gets a little confused.

(Turn to the page on which the list says, "Change the towels in the green bathroom." Read that page, show the picture, turn the page, and show the next picture.) But look what Amelia Bedelia did! She cut the towels. That *is* changing them, isn't it? But do you think that's what Mrs. Rogers meant? *(Repeat for two more instructions.)*

Amelia Bedelia meant well. She just didn't always understand the instructions because she didn't know which meaning of the words to use. There is a verse in the Bible that we might misunderstand in the same way. *(Show the card stock printed with the scripture reference and read it aloud.)* "Love your neighbor as yourself."

Our neighbors are the people who live in the house or apartment next door, right? *(Allow children a moment to answer.)* The people next door *are* our neighbors, but they aren't the only people we can describe with that word. When Jesus asks us to love our neighbors, he's using the word in another way. "Neighbor" can be used to mean anyone we meet. The person who lives in another part of town but rides your school bus is your neighbor. The stranger in line in front of you at the grocery store is your neighbor, too. Any person who you come into contact with, whether you talk to them or not, whether you see that person once or many times, is your neighbor, and Jesus wants us to love all of these people, not just the ones in the house next door.

Now let's look at the word "love." Love is when you see someone special, and your palms get sweaty, your knees feel weak, your mouth feels dry, you're suddenly nervous and giggly, and you don't know what to say, right? *(pause)* Well, that's one of the ways we use the word "love," but it isn't the only way.

Do you love chocolate? Maybe you've said, "I love you," to your grandma. You might love chocolate, but you don't love chocolate the same way that you love your grandmother. You love your little brother and you love your pet, but they are not the same thing. You certainly don't love everyone the way an adult might love a girlfriend or boyfriend. We use the same word, but we mean different things when we say "love."

One reason that love means different things when we're talking about people is that you know some people better than you know others. Another reason is that some people are difficult to even like. It would be hard for you to feel love for everyone in the same way.

Well, that's where some of the confusion comes in. Love is sometimes a feeling, but love is also used to describe action. Jesus isn't telling us to feel anything. He's telling us to do something. When Jesus says to "love your neighbor," he wants us to show love by acting with respect, compassion, and concern, and we can do these things whether we like a particular person or not.

One way we can show love is by telling people about Jesus. Maybe you can invite a friend to Sunday school or tell a new family in your neighborhood about your church. If you meet people who are sad, you can remind them that Jesus loves them and will help if they ask.

What are some other ways can we act with respect, compassion, and concern? We can use polite words, take turns, and share. When we do these things, we show Jesus' love. Can you think of some other ways? *(Allow the children time to make several suggestions.)* These are great suggestions. By practicing these ideas, and others, we can show Jesus' love to all of our neighbors: the ones we stand next to in the grocery store, the ones we sit next to on the school bus, the people who live next door, and to anyone else we meet.

Prayer
Dear Lord,

Thank you so much for this beautiful day, and thank you for loving us. Please help us to remember that everyone we meet is a neighbor, and help us see ways we can show your love to all of them.

In Jesus' name. Amen.

Peggy Parish, *Amelia Bedelia* (New York: HarperCollins, 1963). Used by permission.

Ping-Pong Words

Scripture Reference
A soft answer turns away wrath, but a harsh word stirs up anger.
— **Proverbs 15:1**

Scientific Reference
Snell's law: The angle of incidence equals the angle of reflection.

Materials needed
Board
Ping-pong balls (one for each child if you are going to hand them
    out after the story)
Card stock printed with scripture reference and verse on one side
    and Snell's law on the other
Assistant

Telling The Story
(Introduce your assistant. Ask your assistant to hold the board perpendicular to the floor. Stand three or four feet away and throw a ping-pong ball at a 90-degree angle at the board. The ball should bounce back to you. Ask the children to describe what happened. Stand at a 45-degree angle from the board and throw another ping-pong ball at the board at that angle. The ball should bounce off the board and away from you.) Do you know what just happened? *(Let the children answer.)* What I just demonstrated is Snell's law.

(Hold up the card stock printed with Snell's law and read it to the children.) Snell's law says, "The angle of incidence equals the angle of reflection." This is a scientific way of saying that the way the ball bounces off the board is influenced by the way the ball hits the board. Ping-pong players use this law every time they play. The way they bounce the ball onto the ping-pong table influences the way the ball bounces off, which determines where the ball will go. What does this have to do with the Bible?

Sometimes we get upset with someone we know. When that happens, God wants us to talk to that person rather than gossip with other people. But not just any conversation will do. Imagine that I'm upset with a person named Ignatz. Now imagine that I go to Ignatz and I say *(use an angry voice)*: "Ignatz! You idiot! How could you do something so stupid?" How will Ignatz feel like answering me? He probably will feel like using very angry words, too.

Now imagine that I go to Ignatz and I say *(use a gentle voice)*: "Ignatz, I don't understand something. Can we talk about it?" Now, how will Ignatz feel like answering me? He's much more likely to use gentle words back.

Human beings aren't as predictable as ping-pong balls. It's possible that Ignatz is a calm, mature person who will take a deep breath and count to ten before answering calmly, even if I yell at him. It's also possible that Ignatz will answer me harshly no matter how gently I speak, but I'm much more likely to get an angry answer if I use angry words myself or a gentle answer if I use gentle words.

I learned this in the book of Proverbs. Proverbs was written by Solomon, the wisest man in the world. *(Hold up the card stock printed with scripture reference and verse and read the verse.)* In Proverbs, Solomon says, "A soft answer turns away wrath, but a harsh word stirs up anger." Solomon isn't talking about science, but maybe Snell learned from Solomon. Thousands of years ago Solomon realized that the way you speak to someone influences the way that person speaks back to you. When we use harsh words, we're likely to get harsh words back, just like the ping-pong ball bounces back when I throw it straight at the board. *(Throw the ping-pong ball at the board at a 90 degree angle.)*

When we use gentle words, the anger is more likely to bounce away ... *(throw the ping-pong ball at the board at 45-degree angle)* ... just like the ping-pong ball thrown at an angle.

The next time you find yourself angry at someone, the first thing you should do is pray and ask for God to give you wisdom. Your next step is to either forgive and forget or to go talk to the person gently and try to work things out. Talking calmly is harder than yelling angrily, but remember God is there to help you.

Prayer

Dear Lord,

Thank you for this beautiful day and for giving Solomon the wisdom that he shares with us in the book of Proverbs. Thank you for letting us know that we should use gentle words and for helping us when using gentle words is difficult. Please help us to remember that we can ask you for wisdom, too.

In Jesus' name. Amen.

Optional: Give each child a ping-pong ball to remind him or her of the harsh words and the gentle words.

Science And The Bible

Scripture References
It is he who sits above the circle of the earth.... **— Isaiah 40:22a**

He stretches out Zaphon over the void, and hangs the earth upon nothing. **— Job 26:7**

Genesis 1

Materials Needed
Nine pieces of card stock printed with:
    Isaiah 40:22a and verse
    Job 26:7 and verse
    Genesis 1:1 — astrophysics
    Genesis 1:6 — meteorology
    Genesis 1:9 — oceanography and geology
    Genesis 1:11 — botany
    Genesis 1:20 — ichthyology (study of fish) and ornithology
        (study of birds)
    Genesis 1:24 — mammalogy (study of mammals)
        entomology (study of insects)
        herpetology (study of reptiles and amphibians)
    Genesis 1:26 — anatomy, medicine, psychology
Magnifying glasses, inexpensive, one per child (optional)

Telling The Story
    Once upon a time, a young girl sat in her fifth-grade science class. The teacher talked about evolution, a theory (or guess made after studying) of how everything around us came to be. The teacher told the students that rocks and chemicals floating in space exploded and then spread out, and that some of them came to life. After a while, these living cells changed and became larger animals. The larger animals changed and became other animals that were larger still. The creatures kept changing and changing, until some of them became human beings. The teacher told the students that she knew this was so because science had proven it.

The little girl was confused. So she gathered up all her courage, raised her hand, and when called on, asked, "Ma'am? I thought that God made the world."

The teacher looked over her glasses and responded, "Yes. That's what you talk about at church. That's your religion, but here at school, we have to talk about what really happened."

If you had been in that classroom, you might have felt a little confused, too. Science books and television shows about science usually talk about evolution as if it were fact. When you hear your teachers and people on television say such things, it's easy to think that maybe science and the Bible don't go together. In fact, you might even think that Christians shouldn't study science because science goes against God.

The truth is very different, however. The Bible is a scientifically accurate book. For example, people — even the brightest of scientists — used to think that the earth is flat, but thousands of years before Christopher Columbus sailed, the Bible told us, in Isaiah 40:22a that the world is round. Remember that the *a* means that I'm just reading the first part of the verse. *(Show the card stock printed with Isaiah 40:22a and read the verse.)* "It is he who sits above the circle of the earth" — the earth is round!

A long time ago, many people believed that the earth was floating on a giant ocean or sitting on the back of a giant turtle. What did the Bible say? *(Show the card stock printed with Job 26:7 and read the verse.)* "He stretches out Zaphon over the void, and hangs the earth upon nothing." Our planet isn't floating on an ocean or sitting on a giant turtle. It's floating in outer space where there isn't any water or air. Thousands of years after Job was written, human astronauts took pictures of Earth, and now we can see that it is hanging on nothing, just as Job said.

Human scientists made these mistakes but eventually discovered that what the Bible had already said was true. Why was the Bible able to report what human scientists didn't know? And why is studying science a good thing for Christians to do? *(Let the children give some answers.)* The reason is because God invented science.

That's right. God created everything, including science. Sociologists and archeologists know that you can learn a lot about someone by studying what he made. That's true for God, too. When we study science — something invented by God — we can learn not only about science, but about God himself, too.

So what kinds of science did God invent? Some of them are listed in the very first chapter of the Bible — Genesis, chapter 1. Let's read some of the verses. *(As you read each verse, ask a child to hold up the corresponding card. Have the children line up in front of the congregation so that all can see the cards.)*

(Read Genesis 1:1.) "In the beginning God created the heavens and the earth...." The heavens and the earth? That's *astrophysics*, the study of the characteristics and movements of heavenly bodies. God was the very first astrophysicist because God invented astrophysics.

(Read Genesis 1:6.) "And God said, 'Let there be a dome in the midst of the waters, and let it separate the waters from the waters.' " When God created the world, he created water on the ground and water in the atmosphere. The study of the atmosphere is called *meteorology*, and yes, that's what the weatherman on television studies. God invented the weather, and God invented meteorology.

(Read Genesis 1:9.) "And God said, 'Let the waters under the sky be gathered together into one place, and let the dry land appear.' And it was so." That's *oceanography*, the study of the oceans and everything inside, and *geology*, the study of rock and land formations. God invented oceanography and geology.

(Read Genesis 1:11.) "Then God said, 'Let the earth put forth vegetation: plants yielding seed, and fruit trees of every kind on earth that bear fruit with the seed in it.' And it was so." Does anyone know what the study of plants is called? It's called *botany*. God was the very first botanist, or plant scientist.

(Read Genesis 1:20.) "And God said, 'Let the waters bring forth swarms of living creatures, and let birds fly above the earth across the dome of the sky.' " Here are some new words. The study of fish is called *ichthyology*. Try saying that word: ick- (rhymes with sick), thee- (with a soft th) AH-low-gee. Ichthyology — the study of fish. And *ornithology*, the study of birds. Let's try saying

that word: or-ni- (short I) THAH- (soft th) low-gee. God invented fish and birds, and God invented ichthyology and ornithology.

(Read Genesis 1:24.) "And God said, 'Let the earth bring forth living creatures of every kind: cattle and creeping things and wild animals of the earth of every kind.' And it was so." God invented three branches of science in this verse. He invented *mammalogy*, which is the study of mammals, or animals with hair. He invented *entomology*, the study of insects. He also created *herpetology*, which is the study of reptiles and amphibians. God created all of those animals, and he also created the sciences that study them.

(Read Genesis 1:26.) "Then God said, 'Let us make human-kind in our image, according to our likeness; and let them have dominion over the fish of the sea, and over the birds of the air, and over the cattle, and over all the wild animals of the earth, and over every creeping thing that creeps upon the earth.' " God created human beings. When he did that, he made us special and complex, and so he created many branches of science including anatomy, medicine, and psychology.

God created the world and all the rocks and minerals and plants and animals. He created the human beings, too. When we study what God created, we can learn about him, too. So, remember next time you're studying science at school: you're studying about God. And who knows? Maybe you'll be the next scientist who discovers something that the Bible says is true.

Prayer
Dear Lord,

Thank you so much for this wonderful, amazing, and complex world you created. Please help us to be observant as we study and to discover the clues about you in what you made. Please help the people who don't know about you to discover you, too, as they meet us and as they study your creation.

In Jesus' name. Amen.

Optional: Give each child a small magnifying glass to help them study what God has made.

Something Special To Share

Scripture Reference
Therefore encourage one another and build up each other, as indeed you are doing. — **1 Thessalonians 5:11**

Materials Needed
Card stock printed with scripture reference and verse
Pair of glasses
Toothbrush
Medicine bottle
Toy
Book
Article of clothing
Item of food

Telling The Story
Today, I'm going to tell you something that I imagine you never thought you'd hear someone tell you in church. Don't share. That's right. I'm telling you not to share. *(pause)* Well, actually, I'm not talking about everything, but there are some things that we just shouldn't share. *(Hold up each item for the children to see as you talk about it.)*

One example would be a pair of glasses. Glasses are custom made for each person who needs them. The doctor examines a person's eyes and figures out what vision problems he or she has. The glasses are made to fit that person's head and to correct that person's vision. You might look through a friend's glasses for a few seconds, but if you tried to borrow your friend's glasses for a couple of hours, your friend wouldn't be able to see, and you might damage your own eyes. We just don't share glasses.

I know something else that we don't share: toothbrushes. No matter how much you love someone or how good a friend you are, you don't share your toothbrush. You have bacteria in your mouth, and it gets on your toothbrush. If you let a friend use your toothbrush then he or she would be exposed to that bacteria and leave behind his or her bacteria for you. If some of these are the kind of bacteria that cause disease, the disease could spread. It just isn't sanitary. For that reason, we don't share toothbrushes.

There's something else that we shouldn't share: the answers on a test. You might get together with your friends and study for a test the night before, but if you're at school, in the middle of the test, and you hear someone whisper, "Psst! What's the answer to number twelve?" you don't reply. Test-taking time isn't the time to share. We don't share information during a test.

Maybe you've coughed and forgotten to cover your mouth, and then you heard someone nearby say, "Hey! Don't share your germs, please!" When we cough or sneeze, we cover our mouths so we don't share our germs. If we spread germs, we spread sickness, and we don't want to make anyone else sick. You aren't being selfish if you try to keep your germs to yourself.

Speaking of getting sick, we don't share medicine, either. When you get sick enough to see a doctor, the doctor tries to find out exactly what's making you sick. He or she considers things like what you have, how old you are, how much you weigh, what you're allergic to, and how sensitive you are before prescribing medicine. What works for you might make your friend very sick. In the interest of keeping everyone safe, we don't share medicine.

These are some examples of things that we don't share, and if we sat here a while, I'm sure that we could think of many more things for the list, but instead, let's talk about things that we *do* share.

Toys are things that we share. If a friend comes over to play, you don't make that friend bring his or her own toys. While it's true that the friend might bring one or two toys from home, when you invite that friend over, you share your toys.

Books are another good thing to share. If you've read a really good book, you might loan it to a friend you think will also like it. Maybe that friend loans you good books, too. After you and your friend read the same book, you probably talk about it, too, so not only are you sharing the book itself, but you're also sharing ideas about it.

Clothes are a good thing to share. If you have a friend or a brother or sister who is close to your size, you might let him or her wear one of your shirts that you both like and that person might let you borrow clothes, too.

Sometimes we share food. If you come to a covered-dish dinner at church, you bring some meat, a casserole, a vegetable, or maybe a dessert to share. Maybe at school, you trade things from your lunch box with a friend. If one of your friends forgot his lunch that day, you might let him have part of your sandwich, and when you and a friend go to a movie, you might share a bag of popcorn. Sharing food is an important part of our society, for both health and social reasons.

Have you ever given a friend a ride to church? Maybe one of your parents carpools with someone to work. Or maybe you needed to go somewhere but didn't know how to get there. Someone else who was also going may have invited you to ride along. In order to save gas money, and to keep each other company, we often share rides.

Big jobs are often shared. Imagine if our church needed painting. We wouldn't tell the pastor that he had to paint the building all by himself. We'd plan a workday and everyone who could would come out and help. When a group of people work together, big jobs seem smaller, and that's why we work together and share big jobs.

How about jokes and stories? Have you ever heard a good joke and then you couldn't wait to tell your friends? Did something funny happen at school and you couldn't wait to get home and tell everyone? We love sharing jokes and stories. They help other people get to know us and they make others laugh and feel better.

There are some other things that we, as Christians, can share with each other. We might share our joys — good things that happen to us. We share prayer concerns. If I have a problem, I can tell a Christian friend and know that he or she will pray for me. Sometimes we share Bible verses. If a friend is having a problem and isn't sure what to do, you might read a verse from the Bible that talks about the problem. (Today, you can even email that verse to your friend!) Christian people can also share prayers. Whether we've shared a joy or a concern, when we pray together, we help our friends both in that particular situation and in their overall relationship with God.

Sharing is a way of encouraging. *(Hold up the card stock with the scripture reference and verse on it.)* In 1 Thessalonians 5:11, Paul encourages us to encourage each other. Paul writes, "Therefore encourage one another and build up each other, as indeed you are doing." Just as the people at the church in Thessalonica were encouraging each other by praying and sharing, we should encourage each other by sharing, too. This week, think of a way that you can encourage someone, with a hug, with a prayer, or in some other way that you know will be encouraging to that person and then do it. When we offer encouragement, we know that we're doing one of the things that God wants us to do.

Prayer
Dear Lord,

Thank you for this beautiful day and thank you for all these wonderful Christian friends. Please help us to have a heart like yours and to see opportunities to show each other encouragement. Show us what we can do to be more like you.

In Jesus' name. Amen.

Sometimes, God Says, "No"

Scripture Reference
Ask, and it will be given you; search, and you will find; knock, and the door will be opened for you. — **Matthew 7:7**

Materials Needed
Wristwatch
Card stock printed with scripture reference and verse

Telling The Story

Good morning! *(Hold up card stock printed with scripture reference and verse.)* This morning, I read a verse in the Bible that says, "Ask, and it will be given you; search, and you will find; knock, and the door will be opened for you." And I was so excited! If I ask for something, I'll receive it ... so do you know what I did? I prayed and asked God to send someone at *(insert time here ... 1 or 2 minutes from the current actual time)* to walk through that door and give me one million dollars. *(Insert time.)* That should be right about now. *(Look at watch. Point to door. Stand and wait.)* Right about now. *(Look at watch. Point to door. Stand and wait.)* Maybe my watch is a little fast. Let's wait another minute. *(Point to door. Stand and wait. Look confused. Turn to children.)*

I don't understand it. The Bible said, "Ask, and ye shall receive ..." I asked, but I didn't get a million dollars. I wasn't asking for anything bad. Think of all the good things that would happen if I had a million dollars.

I would give some of it to the church. The church would use the money to help missionaries who are telling people about God, and we know that God wants us to help people who are telling other people about him.

I'd give some of the money to *(insert the name of a medical foundation)*. They're researching a cure for *(medical foundation's research focus)*. God wants us to help people who are sick, and if I donated money to *(medical foundation)*, then I'd be helping the foundation help people who are sick!

I could start a scholarship with some of that money! Scholarships help people go to college, which helps them get good jobs, and with good jobs, they can buy houses and food and warm clothes. God wants us to help people who need homes and food and clothes. If I started a scholarship with some of that money, wouldn't I be helping those people?

So I don't understand it! I had good plans for that money ... plans that would help other people in ways that I know God wants us to help other people. So why didn't I get a million dollars? Well, guess what? I don't know.

God *does* answer our prayers, and sometimes he says, "Yes" to what we ask, but sometimes when we ask for something, God says, "No." Sometimes we *do* know why. If you ask for something that you know God doesn't want you to have, he's going to say, "No." Sometimes we don't know right away. We have to wait until later to learn why God answered a prayer with, "No."

But sometimes we *don't* learn why, at least not on Earth. There will be times in your life when you'll pray for something, and God will say, "No," and you'll have to wait until you go to heaven to learn exactly why.

You see, we human beings think like human beings. God thinks like God. Can you imagine something happening tomorrow? Can you think about something that will happen next year? How about ten years from now? Ten thousand years? It's hard for us to really and truly understand some things because we don't live forever and because we're not nearly as smart as God is!

When I asked God for a million dollars, I was thinking about the good things that I could do with it, but I couldn't know about everything in the whole universe, and I couldn't think about "forever" because I'm a human being. On the other hand, God knows what his plans are. He knows about everything in the entire universe, and he knows everything about "forever." God has pieces of information that I don't have. And maybe the reason God said, "No," is because of something I can't understand yet. The ideas I had for one million dollars might seem like good ideas to me, but God knows what I don't. My ideas didn't fit in God's plans. Someday, God will tell me why he said, "No." He might tell me tomorrow. He might wait to tell me when I go to heaven. Either way, I have to trust that God is in control of the universe. He didn't say, "No," because he doesn't love me. God said, "No," because he does.

Prayer
Dear Lord,

Thank you for this beautiful day and for loving us so much. Thank you for listening to all of our prayers and for always answering. Please help us to remember that you always answer our prayers, that you answer them based on your plans, and that you answer them the way you do because you love us, even when you say, "No." Please also help us to trust you and the answers you give.

In Jesus' name. Amen.

Symbols We Wear

Scripture Reference

... and I by my works will show you my faith. — **James 2:18b**

Materials Needed

Three samples of symbols/identification that people wear, such as an employee name tag, a police officer's badge, a military medal, a Scout badge, a wedding ring, a martial arts belt
Cross necklace or pin
Cardstock printed with the scripture reference and verse

Telling The Story

Today we're going to talk about identification. Identification is something that helps us discover or show who or what someone or something is. Scientists study the characteristics of plants to identify it, and detectives study clues to discover who committed a crime, but did you know that sometimes human beings wear things for the purpose of identifying us?

(Show each piece of identification, explain what it is, how it identifies the person who wears it, and if applicable, what he or she did to earn it. For example: What's this? That's right. It's a wedding ring. I wear it to identify myself as a married person. When people see this ring, they know to call me Mr./Mrs. _____ . Not everyone wears a wedding ring. Not even all married people wear wedding rings, but in our culture, people who want to be identified as married people often do.)

(After each identification piece has been shown, continue with the cross necklace or pin.) What's this? *(Let the children answer.)* That's right. It's a cross. The day I asked Jesus into my heart, someone gave this to me so that everyone would know that I'm trying to follow Jesus and do what he wants me to do, right? Actually, no. I *did* ask Jesus into my heart, and I *am* trying to do what he wants me to do, but no one gave me this jewelry to remember the day. Many stores sell cross necklaces, and anyone can buy one. In fact, some people wear cross jewelry just because they like it, without having any idea who Jesus is!

So if you want to tell people that you follow Jesus, what can you do? You have to remember that it's not what you wear, but what you *do* that identifies you. When you help someone or encourage that person, when you tell the truth, and when you do the right thing even when it's hard, you are *doing* something that Jesus wants you to do. When people look at you, they won't remember what you are wearing. They'll remember that you showed Jesus' love, and then they'll know that you love him.

James tells us that in the book of James. *(Hold up the card stock printed with scripture reference and verse.)* In the second half of verse 18 of chapter 2, James says, "... and I by my works will show you my faith." Although we want to be careful that our clothes don't embarrass Jesus, nothing that we wear will tell people that we're following him. James reminds us with this verse that if we want to be identified as people who love Jesus, we need to show that to people by what we do.

Prayer
Dear Lord,

Thank you for this beautiful day, and thank you for loving us so much. Please help us to remember that people are watching and learning from what we do and that the best way to show them that we love you is to do what you want us to do. Thank you for helping us every day.

In Jesus' name. Amen.

Thankful

Scripture Reference
... giving thanks to God the Father at all times and for everything in the name of our Lord Jesus Christ.   — **Ephesians 5:20**

Materials Needed
Card stock printed with scripture reference and verse
Clothespins, one per child

Telling The Story
(Show a clothespin.) What is this? *(Let the children answer.)* That's right! It's a clothespin. I'm going to tell you about how a clothespin reminded a woman to be thankful.

One day, a woman decided that she was tired of digging through her sock drawer, trying to find matching socks. She pulled out sock after sock, until she found a pair, and then she decided to do something about the mess.

First she went to the store and bought a basket to put her socks in. Then she bought a package of clothespins. At first, she wasn't sure how many clothespins she'd need, but finally decided on a package of fifty. With fifty clothespins, she thought she could match her socks and have a lot of clothespins leftover for crafts or other projects.

She went home, dumped the contents of her messy sock drawer out onto the living room floor, sat down, and sorted her socks. Each time she found a pair, she pinned them together so that the matches wouldn't separate and put the pinned-together socks in the basket.

"My plan is brilliant," she thought, "When I'm done sorting, I'll never have to hunt for socks again. I'll just reach into the basket and grab a clothespin!"

But guess what? She didn't get to finish the job that day, and do you know why? It was because she had more than fifty pairs of socks. Some of them had holes in the heels. She kept those to wear around the house when her feet were chilly, but she didn't want to wear shoes. But most of them were nice socks. There were dark ones for winter and white ones for summer. There were plain ones and socks with flowers that she wore with her jeans. There were argyle socks, striped socks, and socks covered in squiggly lines. She even found one pair of socks that she'd bought several years before but had never worn!

This woman had more than fifty pairs of socks, but she didn't realize it because she took them for granted. In our country, socks aren't very expensive. They're made by machines and sold in bundles at many different stores. If our socks wear out, we just throw them away and buy new ones. Because we don't have to work very hard for our socks and because they're so inexpensive to buy, it's easy for us to forget that not everyone has so many. It's easy to take them for granted and to not be thankful.

But what does the Bible say? *(Hold up the card stock printed with the scripture reference and verse and read it.)* Ephesians 5:20 says, "... giving thanks to God the Father at all times and for everything in the name of our Lord Jesus Christ." God wants us to be thankful for everything, even little things that we might take for granted.

The woman in this story is the woman who wrote this book. She bought more clothespins and finished sorting her socks. Whenever she puts on a pair of socks in the morning, she clips the clothespin to the edge of the basket so she'll know where they are when she does the laundry. And whenever she sees the clothespins on the edge of the basket, she thinks of Ephesians 5:20 and remembers to be thankful for "little things" that she used to take for granted.

I have a challenge for you this week. After our prayer, I'm going to give each one of you a clothespin. Clip it somewhere — like the edge of your pillowcase or on the handle of your toothbrush — somewhere that you'll see every day. When you see the clothespin, say a short prayer and thank God for something that you've taken for granted, like your socks, and then ask God to bless the people who don't have the thing you've taken for granted.

Let's pray.

Prayer
Dear Lord,

Thank you for this beautiful day, and thank you for everything you've given us. Please help us to be thankful for everything, even items such as toothbrushes and socks that we tend to take for granted. Please also show us how we can help the people who don't have the material things that we have. Thank you for guiding us.

In Jesus' name. Amen.

Give each child a clothespin to take home.

Thankful — Two

Scripture Reference
... giving thanks to God the Father at all times and for everything in the name of our Lord Jesus Christ.   **— Ephesians 5:20**

Materials Needed
Calendar
Card stock printed with scripture reference and verse

Telling The Story
(Show the calendar.) What is this? *(Let the children answer.)* That's right! It's a calendar. A calendar helps us keep track of the months, days, and dates during the year. There are twelve months in a year. Let's see if we can name them. Ready? *(Show each month as you lead the children in saying the names in order.)* Very good!

January is the first month of the year. Now, who can tell me something that happens in January? *(Show January. Let the children answer and confirm correct answers. Possibilities include: New Year's Day, Martin Luther King Jr. Day.)*

How about February? It's the second month of the year. What happens in February? *(Show February. Let the children answer and confirm correct answers. Possibilities include: Valentine's Day, Presidents' Day, Groundhog Day.)*

Okay ... how about May? May is the fifth month of the year. What happens in May? *(Show May. Let the children answer and confirm correct answers. Possibilities include: Mother's Day, May Day, Memorial Day, the last day of school.)*

Very good! You know your months! What is the eleventh month of the year? *(Let the children answer. Confirm that November is the eleventh month of the year.)* What happens in November? *(Let the children answer and confirm correct answers. Possibilities include: Election Day and Thanksgiving.)* That's right! Thanksgiving is in November.

One more month. Who knows what the twelfth — or last — month of the year is? *(Let the children answer. Confirm that December is the last month of the year.)* Very good! What happens in

December? *(Let the children answer and confirm correct answers. Possibilities include: Hanukkah, Christmas Eve, Christmas Day.)*

So Thanksgiving, the day we tell God, "Thank you," is in November, the eleventh month. Christmas is really about Jesus, but many people think of Christmas as a time to get presents, don't they? And Christmas comes in December, the twelfth month of the year. Thanksgiving comes before Christmas. In our calendar, telling God, "Thank you," comes *before* getting presents.

Do you think that maybe we can learn something from the calendar? Every year, we celebrate Thanksgiving before we get gifts. That's a good lesson for us. We should always be thankful, but maybe we need to make an extra effort to be thankful *first*. We should make being thankful a bigger priority — and do it first — and make getting things a later priority. In fact, it should be our last priority.

What does the Bible say? *(Hold up card stock printed with scripture reference and verse and read it.)* Ephesians 5:20 says, "... giving thanks to God the Father at all times and for everything in the name of our Lord Jesus Christ." We've read this verse before. It reminds us to be thankful for everything, even things we might not think are special or important. It reminds us also to practice being thankful. When we remember to tell God, "Thank you," even when we aren't sure we need to be thankful, God will help us to see all the blessings that we have. Your challenge this week is to practice being thankful. Tell God, "Thank you," more often than you ask God for more things. Make being thankful a priority. When you do, you'll be amazed at how much you already have.

Prayer
Dear Lord,

Thank you so much for loving us and for taking care of us. Thank you, too, that the calendar shows us that being thankful is more important than getting more things. Please help us to remember this and remember to tell you, "Thank you," every day.

In Jesus' name. Amen.

What Does Heaven Look Like?

Scripture Reference
In my Father's house there are many dwelling places. If it were not so, would I have told you that I go to prepare a place for you?
— John 14:2

Materials Needed
Card stock printed with scripture reference and verse

Telling The Story
Have you ever wondered what heaven looks like? Maybe you've asked people you know and they've described heaven as big and beautiful, with fluffy clouds and angels and harps. Maybe someone has told you that heaven has streets paved with gold and that there are fancy jewels everywhere.

The Bible actually *does* describe heaven as big, beautiful, and full of jewels. Revelation 4:1-6, for example, lists jasper, carnelian, emeralds, and a sea of glass, clear as crystal. Now, you might not think of glass as being special. After all, most buildings today have many glass windows. But remember that in Bible days, glass wasn't so common and that clear glass was very rare. To someone who was living in Bible days, a sea of glass would be very, very special.

Heaven is described as having many beautiful jewels, and that tells us what heaven *looks* like, but what is *being* in heaven like?

Imagine for a minute that one of your friends is coming over for a sleepover. You'll probably clean your room, put fresh blankets and sheets on the guest bed or fix up the family room so you and your friend can "camp out" in sleeping bags. You'll plan your friend's favorite foods for supper and breakfast and hunt up all the pieces to your friend's favorite board game. When someone special comes over, you go out of your way to make sure everything is just right for the visit.

Now imagine that you're going over to a friend's house. Your friend will probably try to make you feel welcomed, too. But when you visit, do you look forward to examining the wallpaper or sitting on the furniture? While it's true that you might be excited about playing with your friend's new toy, eventually that feeling wears off. What you are most happy about is getting to spend time with your friend. *That* is what heaven is like.

(Show the card stock printed with the scripture reference and verse and read it.) The Bible tells us in John 14:2, "In my Father's house there are many dwelling places. If it were not so, would I have told you that I go to prepare a place for you?" Jesus tells us that heaven is like a mansion with many rooms. It's big and it's beautiful, and he's fixing a special place for each one of us. Being in heaven will be like going to visit a friend — your best friend, in fact. Heaven will be big and beautiful and full of very fancy decorations, but what will be most important is that we'll be with our best friend, Jesus, forever and ever.

The next time you wonder what heaven will be like, imagine going to spend the day with your best friend. Then remind yourself that that friend is Jesus and that heaven will last forever. That is what heaven will be like.

Prayer
Dear Lord,

Thank you so much for this beautiful day and for loving us so much. Thank you for getting heaven ready just for us and for being happy that someday we'll get to be there with you. Please help us to remember your love and to focus on you.

In Jesus' name. Amen.

What's In A Name?

Scripture Reference

... and it was in Antioch that the disciples were first called "Christians."   **— Acts 11:26b**

Materials Needed

Card stock printed with the scripture reference and verse

Chalkboard or whiteboard and appropriate chalk/marker and eraser
or card stock sheets printed with the following, one name per
sheet: Farmer, Miller, Johnson, Underwood, Christian

Telling The Story

Have you ever wondered about your name and if it means anything? People who are expecting babies usually spend a great deal
of time trying to think up just the right name. They might decide to
name their new babies after favorite relatives or people in the Bible
whom they admire. Sometimes they buy baby name books so that
they can look up the meanings of names and pick one with a meaning that they like. Around the time that the Pilgrims came to
America, parents liked to name their daughters after characteristics that they hoped their daughters would develop. That's why so
many Pilgrims were named Charity, Hope, and Patience.

Did you know that our last names mean something, too? Today, we usually take the same last name as our parents and many
women still change their last names to their husbands' last names
when they get married. But a long time ago, people didn't have last
names. They just had first names like John or Mary, but as more
and more people had the same name, everyone got a little confused. They had to start adding descriptions to their conversations
so everyone would know who they were talking about. You might
have heard someone say, "I'm talking about William the baker, not
William the cooper." A cooper is a barrel maker. It didn't take long
before these descriptions became part of the name, like William
Baker or William Cooper.

Let's see if you can guess where these last names might have
come from. *(Write "Farmer" on the board or hold up the card*

stock with "Farmer" printed on it. Read the name and let the children guess why a man's last name might be Farmer. Confirm that this man was probably either a farmer or a descendant of a farmer. Repeat with the name "Miller." Write "Johnson" on the board or hold up the card stock with "Johnson" printed on it. Ask why a man's last name might be Johnson and let the children offer suggestions. Confirm that the man was probably the son of a man named John and eventually, as people spoke quickly, John's son became Johnson. Repeat with the name "Underwood." Confirm that the Underwood family probably once lived in a house in or under a forest or woods.)

So we can see that a last name might tell you something about a person's ancestors. If your last name is Farmer, you probably have an ancestor who was a farmer. If your last name is Johnson, you probably have an ancestor whose first name was John.

Because your last name was given to you long before you were born, it doesn't really tell anything about you, but your nickname is different. It's given to you after you're born, after the people around you get to know you. Nicknames often tell us something about the person with the name.

If you met a baseball player named Lefty, what might you think about him? (Let the children offer ideas.) He's probably left handed. If your nickname was Red, what might I guess about you. (Let the children offer ideas.) You probably have red hair. If I heard your mother call you Billy, I'd probably guess that your name was William.

Nicknames can be a lot of fun, but sometimes, nicknames aren't very nice. If someone calls you Four-eyes, or Shorty, you probably wouldn't be very happy, would you? In fact, I'd guess that the person calling you that name didn't like you and wasn't very nice.

Shortly after Jesus died, the people who followed him were given a new nickname, and some of the people using it didn't intend to be very nice. In fact, they were making fun of Jesus' followers. Do you know what that nickname was? (Write "Christian" on the board or hold up the card stock with "Christian" printed on it.) The name was Christian. It can mean "little Christ" or "Christlike" or even "someone belonging to Christ," depending on how it's used. Today, when we use the term, we mean it as a compliment. I might say, "Mary is a good Christian woman," and I'd be saying something nice about her.

But some of the people who started using the term Christian were making fun of Jesus' followers. They were saying things like, "Ha! Ha! He's dead and they're *still* following him. Those silly Christians!" They couldn't believe that anyone would still follow Jesus after he'd died because they assumed that Jesus had failed. (Of course, we know that they were wrong.)

The early Christians, however, took hold of the name and started using it themselves. As they showed Jesus' love to other people, more people came to know him, and eventually, the name Christian started sounding like a good thing!

Just like Jesus takes us when we're sinners and makes clean, beautiful people out of us, the name itself started as an insult, but God made it something beautiful, too.

So what's in a name? Sometimes a lot!

Prayer
Dear Lord,

Thank you so much for loving us and for giving us this beautiful day. Thank you, too, that you can and you do change us for the better. Please help us to remember the story of the name *Christian* and to remember that just as you loved us and patiently help us change, you will do the same for others who love you, too. Help us to see and be willing to do your will.

In Jesus' name. Amen.

What We Do, We Do to Others, Too

Scripture Reference

If any of you put a stumbling block before one of these little ones who believe in me, it would be better for you if a great millstone were fastened around your neck and you were drowned in the depth of the sea. — **Matthew 18:6**

Materials Needed

Paper fan

Card stock printed with scripture reference and verse

Decorative paper, one sheet per child

Printed directions for making a paper fan, one per child, copied from this chapter

Telling The Story

(Sit down next to one of the children and fan yourself with the paper fan. Hold the fan so that it also blows air on the child sitting next to you.) This breeze feels good. I made this fan myself by folding a piece of paper backward and forward. *(Stop fanning. Show the folds.)* It's not very big, but it's just the right size to fan me, and no one can feel it but me. *(Fan again.)* Yes, this is my little fan, and it's fanning just me ... or is it? *(Ask the child next to you if he or she can feel the breeze.)* This little fan doesn't make a big breeze, but it makes enough breeze that I'm not the only one who can feel it.

Sometimes, we're tempted to do things that we know God doesn't want us to do. Do you know what we call things that God doesn't want us to do? *(Let the children answer.)* That's right. When we do something that God doesn't want us to do, we call that *sin*, and sometimes, when we're tempted to sin, we think that maybe it wouldn't be too bad because no one else will be affected. We think, "If I'm the only one who might get hurt, then why can't I do whatever I want?"

The biggest reason, of course, is that God doesn't want us to! Any time we sin, we put something between us and God, and that is something we don't want to happen. We want to stay close to God.

But there's another reason, too. Sin is a little like this fan. Even though I thought no one else could feel the breeze the fan made, someone else could, and sin is like that, too.

Imagine that someone you love is bank robber. That person might think it's okay to rob banks. After all, the bank has insurance to cover its losses, and since he or she is robbing the banks alone, no one else runs the risk of getting caught. That person might *think* these things, but does that mean no one else gets hurt? The people at the bank are hurt. They'll feel stress. They'll be interviewed by the police and have reports to fill out. They may need to clean the bank, they'll have to learn a new security system, and someone might even lose a job. Many people are affected by the insurance payment, too. The insurance rates will go up if the company pays very many claims, or our taxes may go up if the bank is covered by the government.

Even if all of this wasn't true, there is someone else who is hurt by the bank robber's actions. That person is *you*. Remember that we're imagining the bank robber is someone you love. If the bank robber is caught, he or she will probably go to jail. Imagine if the only time you could spend with that person was a few minutes every month in a jail visitor center with guards watching you and maybe glass wall or iron bars between you. Wouldn't that make you feel sad? What if that person was one of your parents? If one of your parents was in jail, he or she wouldn't be able to work and earn money to help support you. What if you didn't have enough food because your father was in jail instead of home, able to go to work?

And even if the bank robber was never caught, that person's actions still affect you. By robbing banks, he or she is teaching you that robbing banks is okay. Instead of helping you learn how to be closer to God, that person is teaching you to sin. The people around us learn by our examples, even when we don't realize that they are!

(Hold up the card stock printed with scripture reference and verse and read it.) Matthew 18:6 says, "If any of you put a stumbling block before one of these little ones who believe in me, it would be better for you if a great millstone were fastened around

your neck and you were drowned in the depth of the sea." Jesus is warning us against leading other people to sin.

So who is hurt by my sin? God is hurt, I am hurt, and so are all the people around me.

Prayer
Dear Lord,

Thank you for this beautiful day and for loving us so much. Please help us to remember that no matter what we do, other people are watching and learning, and that they are affected, both for good and for bad, by what we choose to do. Help us to recognize sin and to avoid it. Thank you for promising to help us follow you, if we'll just ask.

In Jesus' name. Amen.

Give each child a piece of decorative paper and the printed directions to make his or her own fan. Ask them to remember how their actions affect others each time they fan.

To make a paper fan, fold the solid lines toward you and fold the dotted lines away from you to create an accordion pleat.

Willing

Scripture Reference
He responded, "But sir, how can I deliver Israel? My clan is the weakest in Manasseh, and I am the least in my family." The Lord said to him, "But I will be with you...."   **— Judges 6:15-16a**

Materials Needed
Card stock printed with Judges 6:15 on one side and Judges 6:16a on the other

Telling The Story
Have you ever heard the story of Gideon? We find it in the book of Judges, in the Old Testament. At that time in history, the people of Israel were being attacked by the people of Midian. The Midianites would come in and kill the Israelites' animals, steal their food, and burn their crops.

One day a man named Gideon was threshing his wheat. In Bible times, a farmer would toss the wheat plants in the air, letting the wind blow away the parts that couldn't be eaten and letting the edible parts fall to the ground. The problem is that the Midianites would attack anyone they saw threshing wheat, so Gideon came up with a plan. He hid in a wine press, which was a deep hole in the ground used for pressing the juice out of grapes. Gideon probably thought that no one would think of looking for a thresher there!

Of course, someone did: an angel sent from God. The angel told Gideon that God was sending him to rescue the people of Israel from the Midianites! Do you know what Gideon said? *(Show the card stock printed with the scripture reference and verses and read Judges 6:15.)* In Judges 6:15 we read, "He responded, 'But sir, how can I deliver Israel? My clan is the weakest in Manasseh, and I am the least in my family.' "

In our country today, we think of ourselves as residents of our city or citizens of our state or country, but in Israel in Bible times, the people thought of themselves as members of tribes. Each tribe was made of people who were descended from one of Jacob's twelve sons, and each tribe was divided into smaller family groups. Some tribes were thought to be more important than others.

Gideon was a member of the half-tribe of Manasseh, or a descendent of one of Joseph's sons. He told the angel that his family was the least important clan in Manasseh and that he was his parents' least important son. Gideon didn't understand how God could use him when he was so unimportant; what did the angel say? *(Show the card stock printed with the scripture reference and verses and read Judges 6:16a.)* Judges 6:16a tells us, "The Lord said to him, 'But I will be with you....' "

"I will be with you." Why did God choose Gideon instead of a trained soldier? The Bible doesn't tell us exactly. Maybe God was looking for someone creative. If you read the rest of Gideon's story in Judges, you learn that God had an unusual battle plan. A trained soldier might have heard God's plan and said, "That won't work! Here's how we should fight!" But Gideon had already come up with the creative idea of threshing wheat in a wine press. No one else thought of it. Maybe God saw Gideon's creative side and knew that he would see the possibilities in God's plan.

Or maybe God was looking for someone who would trust completely. Military training is no match for God's hand, and God needed someone who would understand that. Whatever the reason, God didn't care that some people thought Gideon was unimportant. God knew that Gideon could do the job if Gideon was willing to trust and follow, and that was what was truly important.

Whenever you're tempted to think that God can't use you because you're "too little," "untalented," or "unimportant," think about Gideon. God saw potential in Gideon because God looks for characteristics that humans sometimes overlook. More importantly, however, God was able to use Gideon because he was willing to be used. Always remember that. God can use you, no matter what anyone else thinks, because the most important thing God is looking for is your willingness to trust and follow.

Prayer

Dear Lord,

Thank you so much for this beautiful day. Thank you for seeing Gideon's potential and his willingness to serve. Please help us to remember that when you see us, you see our willingness to follow first and our other characteristics second. Please help us to remember that you can use anyone, no matter how unimportant we might feel, so long as we trust you. Thank you for your confidence in us.

In Jesus' name. Amen.

The Wise Man Built His House
Upon A Rock

Scripture Reference
Everyone who hears these words of mine and acts on them will be like a wise man who built his house on rock. The rain fell, the floods came, and the winds blew and beat on that house, but it did not fall, because it had been founded on rock. And everyone who hears these words of mine and does not act on them will be like a foolish man who built his house on sand. The rain fell, and the floods came, and the winds blew and beat against that house, and it fell — and great was its fall! **— Matthew 7:24-27**

Materials Needed
Printed music for "The Wise Man Built His House Upon A Rock"
(at the end of this chapter) for the accompanist to follow
Poster with the lyrics to "The Wise Man Built His House Upon A Rock"
The wise man built his house upon a rock (3X)
and the rains came tumbling down.
The rains came down and the floods came up (3X)
and the house on the rock stood firm.

The foolish man built his house upon the sand (3X)
and the rains came tumbling down.
The rains came down and the floods came up (3X)
and the house on the sand went splat!

Telling The Story
(Show the poster printed with the lyrics and lead the children as they sing "The Wise Man Built His House Upon A Rock.") The wise man built his house upon a rock and the foolish man built his house upon the sand. Why are we singing about beach construction?

This is an old song that children have been singing at church for a long, long time, but it isn't really about beach construction. This song uses symbolism to help us understand what Jesus is teaching. Symbolism is when one thing represents or stands for

113

something else. Sometimes, Jesus used an easy-to-understand symbol to help people understand more difficult ideas.

Let's think about the words to this song. The wise man really is a wise man, and the foolish man really is a foolish man.

In both verses, rain came down and floods came up. The rains and the floods represent the problems and temptations that we face. Both the wise man and the foolish man had problems and faced temptations. We all do. It's just a part of life. What do you think the house might represent? *(Let the children suggest ideas.)*

The house is a symbol for our lives. Building a house in this song reminds us of making decisions, reacting to the things and people around us, and living our lives. The two men built their houses in different places, didn't they? This represents living their lives in different ways.

The wise man built his house on the rock. What do you think the rock might represent? *(Let the children offer ideas.)* The rock represents God's teachings. The wise man makes his decisions by checking with the Bible first. When he has a problem, he tries to react in a way that Jesus would want him to. When it rained, when problems came, the man's house was still sturdy and strong.

And what about the foolish man? He built his house on the sand. When the rain came, it washed away and under the house. When he had decisions to make, the foolish man didn't consult the Bible. When his decisions caused problems, his house fell down.

What does this mean for us? If we'd like to be wise, like the wise man, we'll build our lives — that means we'll make our decisions — based on what God teaches us. When we have problems, we'll trust God to take care of us. If we do this, we'll be like the wise man and our lives will be sturdy and firm.

Prayer
Dear Lord,

Thank you for loving us so much. Thank you for helping us through our problems and guiding us when we look to you. Please help us to learn to trust you more and to remember to build our lives on what you teach us.

In Jesus' name. Amen.

The Wise Man Built His House Upon the Rock

Public Domain

The Wise Man Built His House Upon the Rock

116

You Can't Judge A Filling By Its Chocolate

Scripture References

But the Lord said to Samuel, "Do not look on his appearance or on the height of his stature, because I have rejected him; for the Lord does not see as mortals see; they look on the outward appearance, but the Lord looks on the heart." **— 1 Samuel 16:7**

He sent and brought him in. Now he was ruddy, and had beautiful eyes, and was handsome. The Lord said, "Rise and anoint him; for this is the one." **— 1 Samuel 16:12**

Materials Needed

Box of chocolates with mixed fillings
Card stock printed with 1 Samuel 16 (reference only)

Telling The Story

(Open the box of chocolate. Take one out, bite it, and announce its filling. Take out a second piece of chocolate, bite it, and announce its filling.) These pieces of chocolate are very good! From the outside, they very much alike, but when you bite into them, you find out that they are very different. Without the map that sometimes comes with the box, you have to break or bite the chocolate to know what's inside.

Sometimes we judge people by how they look on the outside, but a story in the Bible lets us know that God looks at us differently. *(Hold up the card stock with 1 Samuel 16 printed on it.)*

In 1 Samuel, chapter 16, God told Samuel, his prophet, to anoint a new king for Israel. Anointing is an old practice that involved pouring oil onto the head of a person chosen for a special job. God sent Samuel to the town of Bethlehem, where he was to meet a man named Jesse. Jesse didn't know it yet, but one of his eight sons was going to be chosen as the next king. So Samuel came to town, and Jesse called together his sons.

First, Samuel met Eliab. The Bible doesn't tell us what Eliab looked like, but Samuel was impressed. After seeing Eliab, Samuel thought that he must be the next king. But do you know what God said?

In verse 7, God said to Samuel, "Do not look on his appearance or on the height of his stature, because I have rejected him; for the Lord does not see as mortals see; they look on the outward appearance, but the Lord looks on the heart."

Samuel looked at Eliab on the outside and was sure that he would be the next king, but God told Samuel that he was looking at our hearts.

Finally, Samuel met David. David was the youngest. Usually, the Bible doesn't say much about the way a person looks, but in this case, it does give us some clues. The middle part of verse 12 says, "Now he was ruddy, and had beautiful eyes, and was handsome."

Do you know what ruddy means? It means "red." We don't know if verse 12 means that David had red hair or if he had a reddish complexion from being out in the sun while he was watching the sheep, but the Bible says that he was ruddy and handsome.

The Bible doesn't say this, but it's possible that David was short. Remember that in verse 7, God told Samuel not to consider Eliab's height. Saul, the first king of Israel, was tall, so Samuel and the other people might have expected another tall man to be the new king. When Samuel saw David, he probably thought, "He's young, he's short, and he smells like the sheep he watches all day. He couldn't possibly be the next king."

But remember what else God said in verse 7. God looks at our hearts, not our faces or our heights or anything else on the outside. God knew that David loved him very much and that David was the best choice for the new king. So God told Samuel to anoint David.

Sometimes we treat people just like the chocolates in this box. We look at the outside instead of the inside first. But if we ask, God will help us learn to see the way he sees. Just like this box of chocolate has a "map" to let us know which chocolate is which, God already knows what is inside our hearts and he'll guide us to see the good in each other.

Prayer
Dear Lord,

Thank you so much for loving us and for seeing inside our hearts. Please help us to remember that what is inside the people we meet is much more important than what is outside. Help us to see others the way you see them and to look for the love of you in their hearts.

In Jesus' name. Amen.

Allow each child to take a piece of chocolate from the box.